S0-BHZ-903

The Kingdom of God Today

The Kingdom of God Today

OTTO KARRER

HERDER AND HERDER

1964

HERDER AND HERDER NEW YORK
232 Madison Avenue, New York 16, N. Y.

Original edition "Das Reich Gottes Heute", Ars Sacra, Munich
Translated by Mrs. Rosaleen Ockenden

Library of Congress Catalog Card Number: 64-14108
First published in West Germany © 1964 Herder KG
Printed in West Germany by Herder

Contents

Foreword

THE ESSAYS collected in this book take their origin from recent lectures and group discussions. They have the common aim of bringing the biblical message in its salient aspects closer to open-minded people of our time. Most of those who attended the lectures and discussions were Catholic laymen searching for a more profound knowledge of their faith, but some came from other Christian denominations. The book is therefore addressed to Catholic readers in the first place, but beyond that to Christians at large for whom the Bible is the testimony of Christ's Revelation.

We no longer live in a closed-in world dominated by the Church, but more or less in the Dispersion; and the relationship between believing Christians is very different from that existing half a century ago. We have respect for one another and, in spite of persisting tensions, remain conscious of the fundamental unity of Christians, quite apart from our common mission and responsibility in the face of organized unbelief.

7

It goes without saying that the discussions which followed the lectures – in the Catholic as well as in the mixed courses – served to broaden and deepen the questions treated and have helped me in preparing the written versions. For the theologian and pastor is not a teacher only, but also one who listens and learns, as St. Cyprian and St. Augustine said of themselves. No one has the fullness of Christ for himself alone, and all of us are all our lives learners at the one Master's feet. I am grateful, therefore, to the many who knowingly or un-knowingly have made their contribution.

One Religion among Many

THE QUESTION of what importance should be attached to other world religions, past and present, is one which every thinking person, born and bred in a Christian family, must sooner or later face. Today all classes of people have some knowledge of these religions because of modern education and communication. The Christian cannot put other religions, such as Buddhism or Islam for instance, on a par with Christianity, nor, on the other hand, can he dismiss everything in them as stupid or evil, as completely god-forsaken and of no account in the development of mankind and in its eternal salvation. The Church's teaching is far from demanding such an attitude. But there are many questions of detail which would benefit from a clarification of Christian thinking on the subject.

First we must aim at obtaining an overall view of the history of religion. From the very beginning when it spread from Palestine, Christianity came into contact with different religions. In Athens St. Paul, seeing the signs of religion, said to the pagans: "Wherever I look

I find you scrupulously religious" (Acts 17:22), and he explains that God has given men the desire to seek him and asks: "Would they somehow grope their way towards him? Would they find him? And yet, after all, he is not far from any one of us" (Acts 17:27). We are all the object of God's love, even if we do not all receive the gifts of grace to the same degree.

As children we probably thought of pagans simply as those without faith and Christian missionaries went abroad in order to take the faith to them and with the faith salvation. And it is true that the missionaries have a great deal to accomplish – they have to add to and perfect the rudiments the pagans already possess. But the rudiments are already there. The history of religion offers many proofs of that.

Even in primitive societies the same basic feelings and aspirations can be seen as those at work in more highly-developed religions. These feelings and aspirations reach out beyond the individual; there is a consciousness of a relationship of love and commitment with an absolute being, a reverence for this superior being, the holy one, with the consequent feeling of devotion and trust in all the trials of life. It is true that the more recent researches of men like Jensen[1] and Eliade[2] have shown Schmidt's characterization of primitive peoples to be too optimistic: although there is an unmistakable belief in a supreme deity, spirits, devils, magic and rites of conjuration have

---

[1] *Mythos und Kult bei Naturvölkern* (1951), pp. 129 ff.
[2] *Patterns in Comparative Religion* (1958).

10

a more prominent place in their life; and prayer is chiefly a matter of exorcizing evil spirits, warding off an evil fate or ensuring self-preservation. Surely, however, much the same can be found in the sphere of higher religion, even of Christianity, and it is unfair to blame the religion itself for it. The crucial point is that everywhere there are traces of religious experience, everywhere people are convinced of the manifestations of a benevolent divine purpose, which man is called upon to follow. Early Christian commentators like Justin, Irenaeus, Clement of Alexandria and others had the opportunity of forming their opinion by the actual Hellenism of the time and they too perceived that there was a unity underlying all spirituality. Justin declares:[3] "It is our belief that those men who strive to do the good which is enjoined on us have a share in God; according to our traditional belief they will by God's grace share his dwelling. And it is our conviction that this holds good on principle for all men. Christ is the divine Word in whom the whole human race share and those who live according to the light of their knowledge are Christians, even if they are considered as being godless." Cardinal Nicholas de Cusa, who was well acquainted with non-Christian spirituality from his own observations when he was a papal legate in the East, writes that "God is called by different names, because he has sent different prophets and teachers to different nations".[4] Paul Claudel, who gained his impres-

---

[3] *Apologia* I, 10, 46.
[4] *De pace fidei* 1 (Opera Basil. 1565, 862f.).

sions of the religion of the people from his stay in the Far East, formulated them in an address to the students of Nikko: "Creation as you perceive it is above all a work of God, still pervaded with the divine inspiration. In your country a man cannot enter even the cottage of the humblest peasant without taking off his shoes – with what veneration must men move and go about their business in the vast sphere of the dwelling which the higher powers have given us and the use of which they share with us . . . . The purpose of these temples with the graduations of their different doors and steps is to represent as magnificently as they can the differences between heaven and earth. And what is it that these crowds of pilgrims, who press into your temples with moving eagerness, venerate behind the ever-closed curtains? Some form that melts into the darkness of night or above all night itself, this mystery before which the childlike heart meditates in prayer."

The great religions of the East, free from the rational, analytical and technical approach of the Western mind, are characterized by a total and conceptually synthesized apprehension or intuition of the world. A strong instinctive urge towards the absolute is one of their marks, a vague yet profound and all-encompassing concept of heaven or *tao,* of eternal order and a reverence for the Universal Law which governs everything. Throughout the thousands of years of the distinguished ethical tradition of the Chinese runs the wisdom of Confucius: "Heaven is that which encourages all that is virtuous in me" and the wisdom of Lao-tzu: "The law which man can name is not the eternal law; that law which has no name is the foundation of heaven and earth." In Brahmanism in India the absolute is expressed by an unconscious anthropomorphization as the soul of the world: "He must be honoured as the eternal breath, for in him all are one." The highest wisdom is considered to be interior meditation, which leads to a mystical union with the eternal by means of yoga.

Any philosophical basis for religion, which supports the heart's testimony and tries to protect it from the trials of doubt and despair, is naturally only found in the higher religions, and it is always a question of making the decision between belief and disbelief. In India, as far back as the ancient Vedas, a belief in God in the higher castes led to the mystical philosophy of pantheism. "All in God and God in all" said Sankara, the spiritual counterpart of the mystic Meister Eckhart in the Occident. Similarly Indian Jainism argues in favour of atheism on the grounds that the only possible ethic is one which is pure and has no idea of reward. Yet even in the radicalism of intellectual denials a love of the absolute, of good as the absolute, can be seen, which would never countenance the complete disappearance of spirituality. In no case do rational proofs have the first and last word. Something else is always decisive, in addition to the unconscious influence of the traditions current at the time: in the Bible as in the Indian Bhagavad Gita or the teachings of the Chinese Lao-tzu this decisive factor is called the heart, that is, the receptivity of the inner person for the supernatural mystery of the Holy One.

13

Religious conviction, whenever it can express itself in writing, has the same structure of faith: its origins are in inspiration, in a divine proclamation, its nourishment in the springs of mysticism, its realization in practical love. Faith is the offering of the whole person in all confidence to the mystery of God; it creates within the cult a means of corporate expression and, in proportion to the degree of civilization, as has already been mentioned, produces in conjunction with reason a metaphysical view of life. In order to justify belief in God's existence by intellectual arguments, the philosophical speculations employed go back to the logical principle of sufficient cause. This postulates that the motive for the existence of the finite world lies not in the world itself but in the world as a manifestation of the divine reality. The conscience is both evidence of a spiritual world and an indication of the existence of a divine will governing men. It is not, however, abstract ideas of philosophy which carry the most conviction, whether as introduction to or justification of the believer's position, but experience of life itself, strengthened by the example of outstanding men of religion who, as it were, embody the idea of holiness. They are known as wise men or as saints: men who in everything, in their personal attitude to life as well as their relations with their fellow-men, in their commitment to the forces of good and in their struggle against the evil in the world, renounce all self-love and are influenced purely by the religious motive of offering, of sacrifice, and of self-surrender to the mystery of God. They are clearly seen to be witnesses of and messengers from the Eternal

One and become the prophets, teachers and educators of the world around them. Of them was it said that "it is by her own children that wisdom is vindicated" (Matt. 11:19). A missionary at the Catholic University in Tokyo, who had for years a great deal to do with the Zen Buddhist monks and who had grown to know and admire them, told me of his conviction that these "pagans" possessed the real essence of religious dedication in spite of the pantheistic trend of ideas which they had adopted under the influence of the school. As a result of his investigation of religious witness in other world religions the German missiologist Thomas Ohm O.S.B. wrote a book to which he gave the title *The Love of God in non-Christian Religions* (1950). In his study of the spiritual life of great mystics throughout the world, although particularly concerned with Christian spheres, Henri Bergson came to the conclusion that these sublime and blessed experiences in the human spiritual life could not possibly be based on empty delusion and that in similar imagery they all were trying to describe the Unknown and Unnameable and make it accessible to the world in all its aspects.[5] This could be considered as another aspect of the impression which a reading of Manzoni's hymn for Pentecost made on Goethe: "When men are in disagreement about the manifold events of the time, religion and poetry can reconcile them at a more profound and serious level." Tertullian's meaning was doubtless the same when he

---

[5] *Les Deux Sources de la morale et de la religion* (1932), pp. 243 ff. (Eng. trans. 1935).

investigated the evidence of spiritual life in the world of his time and came to the conclusion that the human soul was "of its nature Christian"; in theological terms he meant that everywhere man's soul was called by the Spirit of God to religious dedication and with the vocation was given the ability to carry it out.

There is a close connection between the study of the history of religion and the problem of the spiritual roots of religious experience. For religious experience is a universal phenomenon – not in the sense that all men are in fact religious, but that the question of religion touches them all, whether they answer it affirmatively in faith or negatively. How can this phenomenon be explained psychologically?

If we first consider the most obvious point we realize that religion is inherited, handed down to us from our ancestors. The form, at least, of the religious life is in general determined by tradition. And although the individual has to decide his personal standpoint as part of his development to spiritual maturity, he cannot and should not easily shed his reverence for what has been handed down to him. All men benefit from those who have gone before them. Religious customs, prayers and cultic rites are handed down from generation to generation. The early formation of good habits and the inculcating of a sense of personal responsibility and a critical ability to distinguish between what is of value and what is not should be the distinguishing marks of the religious education of children. They are, however, too often replaced by lip-service to a vague ideal, which may be no more than an "extra" – for instance, the Communist ideal of the brotherhood of man. But the religious element rarely disappears altogether and where it does human existence feels the loss. The conflict between piety and freedom is one which informs the life of every individual.

Among so-called primitive peoples tradition is both the instrument of mediation and the most important basis for religion: it is one source of the community feeling of a race or people. "God revealed himself to our forefathers", is a saying amongst these peoples and he still manifests himself in the thousand-year-old rites of initiation for their youth and in strange cultic symbols like the totem. This is the way in which peoples who otherwise have no sense of history, no monuments, records, archives or schools, preserve a sense of continuity with their past. They live in the religion of their fathers. The opinion formerly common among Western scholars, that the strength of the community feeling among primitive peoples prevented the development of any individual viewpoint, is now recognized by ethnologists as based on a misconception. P. Radin,[6] who is free from any apologetic interest in the matter, has shown that among primitive peoples too the collective pressure of the tribe's traditions is far from being simply and unconditionally the sole influence, but that they too are composed of believers, sceptics and searchers, just as there are in their midst people of melancholic or of sanguine disposition, introverts and extroverts, those governed by reason and those governed by emotion.

[6] *Die religiöse Erfahrung der Naturvölker* (1951).

A few examples will, however, show how great the influence of tradition is among all classes, high and low. D. J. Wölfel[7] has shown of the pre-Indo-Germanic peoples in Europe that the nobles of the tribe committed suicide voluntarily, as a matter of honour and religious custom, when their chief died: they followed him into the tomb as a sort of consecration to the super-ego. The changes which can be brought about by a politico-social totalitarianism by means of educational pressures, we know from our own present-day experience. As far as past history is concerned W. Koppers[8] has made out a convincing case for the fact that in the development of religion in India the people's initially personal belief in God was deliberately turned by the ruling class into an impersonal fatalistic philosophy. There is no danger of any appeal being made to the dignity of man in the name of the living God, if the masses are educated to a passive resignation.

In general, however, religious education has great positive significance for man's elevation above his earthly destiny. For hundreds of years the millions of followers of Islam have been formed from their early youth by the sayings from the Koran which they learn by heart, by the observance of the hours of prayer and by religious practices. Sunna, that is religious practice, regulates their lives and much that is human mingles with what is sacred.

[7] In F. König, *Christus und die Religionen der Erde* I (1951), pp. 161 ff.
[8] In F. König, *op. cit.*, II, pp. 665 ff.

It is due to the religious education given from generation to generation that the Muslim patients in hospitals, as a nurse told me, almost all show a resignation to the will of God and a peacefulness of mind, by which the Christian cannot fail to be edified. "The greatness and wretchedness" of man, to use Pascal's characterization, is to be found in the spiritual history of individuals as well as in that of religious groups. We read in St. Paul's second letter to Timothy of a remarkable example of the handing on of grace (1:5): "I long to see thee again, so as to have my fill of joy when I receive fresh proof of thy sincere faith. That faith dwelt in thy grandmother Lois, and in thy mother Eunice, before thee; I am fully persuaded that it dwells in thee too." St. Paul affirms here the powerful influence of upbringing on the individual's attitude to religion.

Nonetheless, human limitations in general persist, although religious tradition imparts the values of faith. For centuries the churches in our various countries have been calling people to the one eternal God, but their call is not to one Church but to many. They do not pray together, although they admit their belief in one and the same God, in one and the same Lord, Jesus Christ, for they have been brought up to be in conflict. Emotions, which are inherited and which take root long before any enlightening of the intellect, dictate the direction to be followed by growing minds and determine the separate convictions with their appropriate sympathies and antipathies. To love is to know; without love there is no possibility of real knowledge. It is obvious to everyone who gives thought to the matter that it would make for a better understanding and relationship between separated Christians and contribute to the healing of the scandal of reciprocal coldness, if we consciously made the effort to purify the influence of the group, to nourish our spirituality and cultivate our potentiality for justice and love and to free ourselves from prejudices.

From this discussion of the most obvious aspect, the outer form of religious belief as it springs from tradition, it is clear that the psychological side of religious feeling has been only partly dealt with, for it has deeper roots than mere form. If it sprung only from tradition and habit, it would be easily discarded: generations grow apart and youth goes off in a new direction. The reason for the persistence of religious feeling, even where it comes into conflict with a counter-tradition, is that it is rooted deep in the spirit of man. Present-day psychology supports this view. There are in man depths of which he is unconscious, archetypes of the soul, innate dispositions and tendencies which express themselves in emotions, images, aspirations and ideas and which all have as their ultimate aim the eternal Thou. The direction of man's existence would seem to be predetermined. If the *imago,* the unconscious ideal of the *Thou* which every man has within him, were only a sublimated form of sensual love, religious feeling would die on the experience of a great human love. This does not happen; it is precisely those who do love another human being who discover, as the German poet Eduard Mörike said, that no one on earth can ever belong as fully to another person as he would wish.

Man's fundamental relationship remains one which involves his capacity to stretch far beyond his own limits and those of his earthly counterparts. For all human I-thou relationships are at the deepest level a reflection of and preparation for that other love for the eternal Thou. This is the biblical interpretation, as it is found in the poetry of the Canticle of Canticles and the theology of St. Paul's epistle to the Ephesians. The psychologist C. G. Jung found that there is in the human soul the secret image of Christ, the longing for a redeemer figure, as the unconscious leitmotive of the music of human existence.

From a theological viewpoint it is worth considering whether the expression "religious disposition" does not require some qualification. Historical man is fallen man and it would be a contradiction of revelation to suppose him capable of accomplishing his own salvation without God's self-manifestation. But God, as St. Paul said to the Athenians, has given men the desire to search for him. He is love itself – even to fallen man. "The knowledge of God is clear to their minds; God himself has made it clear to them" (Rom. 1:19). Through God's manifesting himself, through man's enlightenment and inner contact with him, God's call is made possible; and when man opens himself to the light which "enlightens every soul" (John 1:9) his progress towards salvation has started; when, however, man in the self-exaltation of original sin opposes God's power, which draws all to him, he incurs God's judgment. Nonetheless, the remedy is always there, for God always "makes his sun rise on the evil and equally on the good"

21

(Matt. 5:45) and he is ever ready to repeat his call. The light "shines in the darkness, a darkness which was not able to master it" (John 1:5). Man's existence may be threatened by the darkness but it is not simply overwhelmed by it. For he who is always present will not desert mankind – or so Martin Buber interprets God's revelation of himself in the thorn-bush: "All things thou lovest nor holdest any of thy creatures in abhorrence." What appears psychologically as a search for God is, in fact, a being-drawn-towards-him by him in whom all have their existence. He shows himself to all and "it is his will that all men should be saved" (1 Tim. 2:4). From time to time theologians like Karl Barth refuse to accept the idea of a general revelation or manifestation from the fear that thereby the one and only salvation in Christ would be put in question. As M. Lackmann has pointed out it is a contradiction to say on the one hand that "the heathen also have always sinned no less responsibly against God: they have sinned against the truth which they too knew so well," and on the other hand to maintain that the apostle gives them witness of the truth *only* "in and with the proclamation of the gospel", that is in their meeting with the Christian mission.[9] For what a man does not know, cannot be held against him.[10] And "where is it written in the Old and New Testament that the reality of the merciful or wrathful God is only revealed in the efficacy of the law and of the gospel? Is his efficacy restricted

[9] K. Barth, *Church Dogmatics* (1936), II, 1, p. 120.
[10] *Op. cit.,* I, 2, p. 306.

to the narrow bounds of the Church and those who come into contact with her?"[11] According to St. John (chap. 1) the light shines in darkness and to believe that the light is no longer shining and that only darkness remains is "a scepticism to which no biblical witness has ever considered subjecting God the Creator and Father of Jesus Christ and his creation".[12] Thus it is in the line of Christian tradition to think that it is not only a natural knowledge which precedes the Christian faith among religious people of non-Christian lands, but a spiritual disposition which has the characteristic qualities of religious dedication and "which stands fundamentally on the same level as the Christian does", the level of a revelation in which God manifests himself and man has to listen intelligently and then to believe. For "how can this relationship with God be described except by being categorized as 'faith' and the person as 'a believer'?" It is not merely a question of rational thought, which concerns our relationship with ourselves and with inanimate objects but not with God, but of a faith which has to be judged critically, which is wayward and imperfect, but which has been awakened and kept alive in all its positive aspects by the Spirit of God. From the theological side it would be difficult to say anything against the opinion of religious psychologists who view the religious movement in mankind in the final event as a mystical process, in so far as those moved by God themselves attribute their

[11] M. Lackmann, *Vom Geheimnis der Schöpfung* (1952).
[12] *Op. cit.*, p. 188.

experience to an illumination or revelation, a mystical contact of which the effect in the life of the soul shows itself as contrition, the longing for salvation, trust in God's grace, and impulses of love and peace.

It is therefore far from surprising that both writers on sacred history and psychologists find certain common characteristics among all forms of religious feeling and that these are similar in all religions. According to Friedrich Heiler's evidence, prayer as the expression of faith, adoration, hope of salvation and love is to be found in all religions. Likewise R. Pettazzoni has shown that confession or similar absolutory rites and sacrifices exist in almost all cults. It is true that there are important differences. In the great world religions, such as those found in India and China, the stress is on the experiencing of dependence and tranquillity in the face of the Eternal; instead of the dialogue of prayer there is absorption, instead of the intimacy of a personal friend, the impersonality of a superior being. Nonetheless, all religions intermingle and influence one another and not infrequently, in movements like the Indian Bhakti mysticism or the religion of the Buddha Amida or in Islamic spirituality, the devotion is of such an ardour that one cannot deny it has all the marks of the love of God.

Finally we come to the question of what distinguishes the Christian element in the religious feeling common to all mankind. There are three possible explanations as Cardinal König[13] has pointed out: 1. All religions are equal;

[13] *Op. cit.,* III, p. 735.

they are all fundamentally of the same value or lack of value, even if there are differences of degree between them or if Christianity represents a particularly valuable contribution. This is the viewpoint of non-Christian writers. 2. Christianity alone rests on a true Revelation and everything outside Christianity is to be considered purely as error, corruption, and the work of the devil – according to the exponents of dialectical theology. 3. All non-Christian religions, when compared with Christianity, share with it common values given by God; historically and ideally they are a preparation for Christianity and some of the richness and greatness of the Christian Revelation is adumbrated in their values and ideals. This is the eternal will of God for man's salvation; for God revealed himself from the beginning and his spirit fills the earth and points forward to Christ, the first-born before all creation, the focus and the fulfilment.

In explanation of the third viewpoint it should be pointed out that an absolutely unbiassed comparison of religions could not lead to any assured conclusion and would from the start be an illusion, since, unconsciously yet inevitably, personal criteria would be used. One person values speculative truth for itself, another its practical application; one values forgiveness, the other sanctification; one has a preference for communal worship, the other for the mystical personal relationship between God and the soul. Taking into account human criteria and unconscious influences on them, as also the philosophically or psychologically possible relativism, which considers all aspects of the one divine mystery as of equal value – any decision

25

can only be taken from a religious angle, as a consequence of belief in an authority which can enforce acceptance of the call "Come and follow me" and "You, therefore, must go out, making disciples of all nations", because it is a direct call in God's name. In this way Christ brought his influence to bear on history. The distinguishing mark of Christianity, its individual character in contrast with its predecessors, lies in its fulfilment of our salvation, that is its unifying and rectifying of otherwise disparate merits in the person of Jesus Christ, through whom the mystery of God speaks and acts directly and with the full force of commitment. All have received grace through him, whether they know his name or not; but those who have recognized him and followed him in faith have received "grace answering to grace" (John 1:16). For the Christian there is no greater revelation on earth and there is no higher vocation for man than adherence in faith to the Son in whom God himself was well pleased and participation in his mystical Body.

Seen for themselves the religious systems outside the Messianic line of Revelation, outside God's covenant from Abraham to Christ, are characterized by a mixture of divine and human elements, of truth and error, of sanctity and corruption. All truth as such is from God, even if it is only a few scattered beams of light from the Logos; error and confusion are always the work of man. When a man comes into contact with a higher phase of revelation, he is faced with a new decision, one which did not previously concern him. Previously he was the heir of a system, of a part-truth, of a mixed tradition of wisdom. Even in this tradition there was a confrontation with God, who manifested himself to the individual in creation, in history and in the conscience. Confronted with God's manifesting of himself, man was able from the beginning to acknowledge his own failure, the hidden selfishness of his heart, his secret resistance to God's will, that conflict of which St. Paul speaks in his epistle to the Romans (Rom. 7:14–25), where he depicts the condition of the man, bound by original sin, who is faced with the experience of salvation in Christ. Right from the beginning man could and can know of the promise of grace and have recourse to mercy. The New Testament names only *one* condition of salvation for all men: faith in salvation from God (Heb. 11:6). It would be an historical error to believe that faith in grace and mercy was not possible until the Christian era. It is only necessary to open the Bhagavad Gita or read the Ancient Egyptian prayers of repentance or learn of the Buddhist belief in a saviour to realize how deep the consciousness of God's grace and mercy can be rooted even in pagan traditions.

The missionary's task is to relate what has been effected by the spirit of God in the flesh of human traditions to what is already there. St. Paul in Athens, as earlier in Lycaonia (Acts 14), is the Christian example for this and he is unmistakably continuing in his theology the teaching of the book of Wisdom (Wisd. 13:6; Is. 55:5f.). Here it is taken for granted that God wishes men to find him and that he has always called men to him. They can either refuse or accept his offer – yet his grace remains always open to those who did not follow the first call. No one, even if he is a Christian, is justified by his own perfection. St. Paul

27

assures the pagans that in spite of their denial of him God "has not left us without some proof of what he is" and "has shut his eyes to these passing follies of ours" (Acts 14:17; 17:30). St. Augustine is admittedly not of one mind on the subject; nonetheless, as far as God's shutting his eyes to human errors is concerned in his commentary on Psalm 84 he maintains: "Every human being learns the tongue of the environment in which he is born. He thinks and lives in accordance with his environment. How could a child brought up among pagans not worship a stone statue if this is the cult of his parents? From their mouth he heard the first sounds of speech, he sucked in the error even with his mother's milk." Dominating the unskilled workers in present-day Soviet society – the class between state officials and the former peasantry – appears to be a primitive struggle for life tainted by suspicion of their rulers; while religion appears to have been reduced to occasional strange stirrings and external observances left over from the past. We might recall Cardinal Billot's theory that a section of humanity always remains at a stage of spiritual childhood. Yet it would require temerity to judge with our human sense of proportion what secrets of divine mercy are hidden in these obscure emotions, or how much or how little necessary for salvation with him who "knows all things", "with whom there are no human preferences" (Col. 3:25) and who "has power to raise up children to Abraham out of stones" (Matt. 3:9). In Cardinal de Lugo's[14] view God's way of salvation is such that

---

[14] *De fide* (1646) XII/3.

scattered beams of the divine light are efficacious even in the most unfavourable conditions and those who are called and who are ready are nourished spiritually, under the influence of the divine light, by those elements in their tradition which embody all that is true, good and holy, while they retain an immunity from all the elements of corruption.

According to this way of thinking the Christian religion does not represent the first possibility of salvation for those whom its preaching reaches, but it reveals to them "the unknown object of their devotion", the "fulfilment". "There have been many prophets and just men who have longed to see what you see" (Matt. 13:17). The difference between religions consists in the fact that the "heathen religions are a true religion corrupted; the Jewish a true religion dead; and Christianity the true religion living and perfect".[15] Christian and non-Christian religions have a common and supra-historical source: God himself who illuminates men, touches their hearts and draws them to him. All religion and all spirituality is, as far as its merits are concerned, from God, the Father of light, from his breath which awakens and animates – in spite of the humanizations and corruptions which are at all times the work of man, the dues of the flesh. What distinguishes the Christian religion is its historical origin in direct descent and formation from the temporally tangible source of salvation, from the incarnation of the Eternal Being himself. Through him the religion of perfection came into

[15] J. H. Newman, *Parochial and Plain Sermons* V, p. 18.

existence; elsewhere the signs of God are more or less scattered beams in the darkness, but he is the "Light of the world", the image of divine love. Distinctions as to value where non-Christian religions and spirituality are concerned are distinctions in the distribution of grace, of which God alone disposes. In so far as all men, even though they are unaware of it, participate in salvation through God's incarnation, there is nothing to separate all believers, for there is "one God and Father of all" and *one* Saviour of all and *one* omnipresent Spirit, "the Breath of Life". In acknowledging Christ, Christians know themselves as having been especially chosen, without any merit of their own – but they do not regard others as pariahs, shut off from God's grace because they were born in Tokyo or Benares or Mecca instead of in Jerusalem. For this reason Christians offer, in response to St. Paul's plea, "petition, prayer, entreaty and thanksgiving for all mankind ... since it is God's will that all men should be saved" (1 Tim. 2:1, 4).

Thus the supernatural call to salvation is a necessity for all men and this seems to us to have biblical roots. If Jesus said of the faith which he found in the pagan centurion: "And this I tell you, that there are many who will come from the east and from the west, and will take their places in the kingdom of God with Abraham and Isaac and Jacob" (Matt. 8:11), then the call to salvation is given a universal stamp through the grace of God which can awaken faith in all men. According to tradition the Magi from the East were pious pagans and have always been venerated as such in Christendom. In the Old Testament Job is described as a pious pagan who, fearing God and doing good, could resist evil and know salvation. Thus we may take St. Augustine's observations on the membership of the mystical Body of those who prepared the way for the Messiah, as applicable to all those who love God and who are not Christians: "The apostle calls head and body together the one Christ: you are Christ's body and members, all of you, not only here but across the whole world, not only now but I should say from Abel the just to the end of the world, whenever just men make their pilgrimage through life. This entirety is the body of Christ and the individuals are its members."[16] Cardinal Newman also maintained that all religions had God as their common originator. From the beginning of time, he held, this creed of mankind was the work of a supernatural principle that initiated as well as perfected.[17]

To talk of a purely natural religion, of a natural love of God, of a natural mysticism in the non-Christian spheres, is not an explanation which can be seriously developed. There is no purely natural tendency of man, no purely natural order or level of human existence. According to Scripture, God's intention is to lead all men to salvation; all are descended from Adam and so they are not in the natural state but in the state of original sin. Those who do not follow the call addressed to them are not children of nature but children of sin; those who do follow it are made children of grace. As Karl Rahner says: "In spite

[16] *Sermons,* 341.
[17] *University Education* (1852), p. 161.

31

of their newness Christ and his Revelation are not the first in time to bring the supernatural into the world, although all that is supernatural depends upon him. . . . So it is Revelation which first throws light on the half or even completely concealed supernatural factor in pre-Christian and non-Christian religion and philosophy, which cannot be regarded as some sort of purely natural religion or purely natural speculation, nor again as religion and philosophy which have been corrupted in some purely natural way."[18] M. Lackmann's reference to the inner continuity of the Credo is also significant: "Both Catholic and Protestant theology have always maintained the creature's communion with God as the first article of faith and as a prerequisite for the second and third articles, in obedience to Scripture. Any denial of this (as in the works of Karl Barth) has not only the consensus of Christian opinion against it, but over and above this makes the biblical content of Revelation into a mystical and secret doctrine or mystery religion undervaluing and rejecting the world, in which the Gospel is no longer God's helping support of his creature and his world but their negation. The Gospel of Jesus Christ is, however, God's affirmation, not his rejection of creation, history and natural life."[19] The Old Testament books of Wisdom are based on the interchange of ideas with Hellenism. Even among the formidable Rabbis of the Talmud with their hatred of foreigners, there were some who differen-

---

[18] Karl Rahner, *Theological Investigations* I (1961), p. 81.
[19] M. Lackmann, *op. cit.,* p. 271.

tiated between unbelieving and pious pagans. As far as early Christendom is concerned, it is sufficient to point to the attitude, both in theory and practice, of the Fathers of the Church towards the wisdom of the Greeks. St. Basil's "Address to Young Men", for example, is prefaced by St. Clement of Alexandria, who in his *Stromata* regards the ancients as a sort of third Testament beside the Old and the New, as a work of Providence and a preparation for "wisdom in the spirit of Christ". The Creator and the Redeemer are one and the same God and his works are directed in the beginning, now, and always by the same great plan of merciful love.

The question now obtrudes whether St. Paul did not paint the moral depravity of the heathens in the first chapter of his epistle to the Romans in such colours as are irreconcilable with the presumed presence and efficacy of grace – it being borne in mind that he did not know of a purely natural order of existence. First of all it must be said that he is speaking of the typical pagan, as previously of the typical Jew, and the basic idea behind each is that no one should boast of himself. The Jews in general, the Jew as a type, is hardly better treated by St. Paul. If the pagans are guilty through their depravity, so are the Jews through their arrogance. But God remains God and even if the sinner experiences his anger and his judgment, he is and remains in essence, Love. In the second chapter of the same letter St. Paul adds: "There will be affliction then and distress for every human soul that has practised wickedness, the Jew in the first instance, but the Gentile too; there will be glory and honour and peace for everyone who has done good, the Jew in the first instance, but the Gentile too. There are no human preferences with God"(Rom. 2:9–11). He has let all men incur guilt, only to include them all in his pardon (Rom. 12:32) and lead all to salvation who will be led by him. For Abraham, the father of faith, and the pious believers who are described in the epistle to the Hebrews (chap. 11) cannot be amongst those Jews condemned by St. Paul for their arrogance. Nor can "Job dwelling in the land of Hus", nor the Magi with their gifts, nor the centurion with the faith which was not found in Israel, nor Socrates who died for the sake of his conscience, be among those pagans whom St. Paul condemns because of their vice and corruption. Everywhere God's grace selects those who, when moved by his spirit, free themselves from their egoism and follow in faith the impulse of the Divine and the Good. Such men have a share in the kingdom of God and are members of the Body of Christ, of the Church and of the communion of saints.

Theologically "the absoluteness of Christianity" needs explanation; the term is taken from Hegel and it would be better in a theological context to speak of the Christian Revelation, as does the New Testament, as a fulfilment, as a fullness of the divine merits of salvation, as grace upon grace. And if others too receive grace from the one source of salvation – "Must thou give me sour looks because I am generous?" (Matt. 20:15.)

Man is tempted throughout his life wherever he may be by a persistent inclination towards making himself the secret focus and standard by which to judge the rest of the world. This temptation permeates everything, even the

34

religious life of all religions. It is a temptation which attacks the pious man: to seek communion with God and yet avoid doing his will. It runs through all human thought and aspiration, through the prayers and forms of worship of mankind in general, as through the history of Christian devotion and Catholic mysticism: human corruption must be taken into account even in experiencing sanctity. Even Christ himself trusted in the last resort not in his own perfection, but in God's compassion.

To the communion of his disciples through the ages, to his Church, Christ has promised his constant presence through his Spirit in word and in sacrament and it is from these sources that the Body of Christ draws its sustenance and grows to the maturity of Christ to the degree that it lives through Christ with God the Father *in unitate Spiritus Sancti*, in the unity created by the Spirit of love. Theologians tend to debate the exterior marks of the Church as a visible body: the truth of its teaching, the sacraments, the ordered hierarchy, and in doing so they describe the outward appearance of the divine structure. Its life, however, is an interior life; the Spirit is the Church's soul and what bears witness to its inner life is, above all, love modelled on Christ's love. The early Church called herself simply love, and the world said of her: "See, how these Christians love one another!" This is the spirit which should animate any missionary encounter with believers in the first stages of Christian life, with those who possess only part of the Christian truths. Such an encounter should have in it no element of arrogance or contempt. Rather it should be modelled on the Chinese priest who once told me that he

35

believed himself to have been given two tasks by God as part of his priestly vocation: to show his Western brothers not to despise the traditional wisdom of his forefathers and to bring to his own people the light of Christ.

"The light shines in darkness, a darkness which was not able to master it" – here is the key to religious history. The history of mankind is the history of religion and the history of religion is the history of salvation. Seen from beneath it is a carpet which looks only like a twisted mass of threads, a terrifying picture of the human situation, if it is even a "picture". But our view is only of the underneath, of what is humanly visible, and we do not see the picture from the right side, from above, where God's spirit weaves the history of man in secret. The glad tidings of Christ are the realization and manifestation of God in the world as love itself. *Omnis homo mendax* (Ps. 115:2): no man can be trusted; and yet *videbit omnis caro salutare Dei* (Luke 3:6): all mankind is to see the saving power of God.

What of the unbelievers that there always are, whatever religion is being preached? This is a difficult problem, and it weighs particularly heavily where the unbelievers are in the Christian environment of the West and are perhaps to be found among the friends and family of Christians. "The man who does not believe is already rejected" (John 3:18), Christ said. But we must guard ourselves against the Pharisaical spirit of judging other people harshly. Many of those who seem unbelieving are far from lacking all religious traits. Perhaps they are sceptical about the far from impressive form in which religion was first presented to them. For a great deal always depends on the sort of introduction, even on the human sort, the person who represents religion to them. Others are claimed by the worries of everyday life; they have not had much time up till now to devote to thinking about religion and it takes time, they say. Others are simply indifferent, uncommitted or antipathetic. Religion is said to be an invention of human longing for a God.

Unbelievers are like blind people. How spiritual blindness happens is not something which can ever be morally judged, as far as actual human beings are concerned, but only psychologically conjectured with every reservation and without any condemnation. Those who are blind are sufferers – in any case they lack something, from an objective point of view perhaps even the one essential thing. It is their misfortune. Those of them who are philosophers speak of an existence lived in darkness and of great fear. This is some indication of profound suffering. There are men among them who came to believe later in life, including many who are famous. They speak of their former condition as a time when "it had not dawned on them". Was there then no trace of any religious feeling in them at that time? Was nothing latent of what later dawned on them? I shall never forget a conversation I had with a convinced materialist. He was by birth a Protestant, although in fact without any religion even in his youth and brought up by his family in that way; even confirmation had no effect on him. But he was a fine man and loved by his family; his wife was devout and his children brought up as Catholics. "Religion suits them – they need it" he would say, as though he had no aptitude for it himself, as if it were like being unmusical; he couldn't help it and could not do something merely in order to conform, he said. I did not trouble him again on the subject and soon after he died. I have no doubt personally that his soul is at rest, for I trust in God to have room in the eternal mansions for such people. Just as there are people for whom it seems that any religious feeling has been relegated to a subsidiary position, perhaps to a system of concepts and laws in which they seek peace of mind and a feeling of being justified, there are also others for whom, as Bishop Sailer[20] pointed out, what is sacred presents itself for worship veiled in a sense of duty and these people find it impossible to involve themselves in a cult or in anything which might seem like a dialogue with God, even if they envy others for their ability to do so. All men are inadequate, all are dependent upon grace, and what is impossible in the human sphere, will not be impossible in the divine.

There are others who deny God and who try to justify their objections, in such a way that their emotion can be sensed. This indicates a spiritual difficulty and should excite our sympathy. The experiences they have had of believers are often reason enough to make them keep their distance. Their opinion is that religion is in reality an escape from humanity into the heaven of an egoistic desire for happi-

---

[20] J. M. Sailer, *Werke,* VIII (Sulzbach, 1830), p. 30 f. Sailer's original text is worth quoting in full: "Especially noteworthy is the phenomenon that men who differ in their idea and conception of God, are reunited in their awareness that the divine presents itself veiled for our adoration. So the conscience can be seen as a unifying point for all systems."

ness. And in addition there is this claim to possess absolute truth, this arrogant judging of others who think differently and who thought it out for themselves – not to mention the disunity of Christians among themselves, which has lost them any possibility of being trusted by thoughtful men, and in addition their denigration of temporal values, their depreciation of this life and their low opinion of natural knowledge, of the cultures of this world, of human love – all in the name of religion! We owe it to ourselves and to these others to bear in mind to what an extent man's religious life is in a state of constant trial and temptation and exposed to the danger of corruption. For everything which has just been quoted is not in reality said against religion, nor against God, but against the way in which men actualize their religion. If faith is thought above all to be the approbation of clauses in a philosophical system or way of life or an adherence to certain ideas and concepts, faith in the biblical sense, and with it what is most truly religious, is obscured or hidden altogether: that is, the personal relationship with the eternal Thou, the surrender of the soul to the call of the Lord God, to the "one thing that is necessary". The man seeking God forms his conception of religion from the form in which he sees it, in which often what is secondary stands in the place of the primary. The faith in which is our salvation is, according to the gospel, the existential faith, the trustful surrender to the all-saving and all-helping God, and all else has its importance only in the degree to which it serves this basic relationship with the eternal. As for the denigration of temporal values in the name of religion, Christ himself, the prototype of holiness,

39

is free of it, whatever may have been said or presented in a way that could be misunderstood in the course of history. The greatest part of his life was devoted to ordinary work for his family and to his earthly occupation and he was not less the Son in whom God was well pleased, in doing this work than he was when he preached to the multitudes or died on the cross. He loved nature and men, precisely those men who are unloved and who are troubled in themselves, the sinners. He had friends, both men and women, and thought highly of human affection: for him the perfect marriage is so great a grace that it can only be comprehended "by those who have the gift". The same words are used to commend a religious vow of chastity. It is certain that many of those who say they cannot stand "pious people" would love him, the prototype of all that is holy, if they were to come face to face with him.

First Steps in the Encounter with Christ

OUR FIRST notion of Christ may have derived from the pictures which Christian parents and teachers use to introduce children to sacred things. It is in early youth that the foundations of a person's later development are laid. In general, what the mother then imparts to the child in the religious sphere is decisive for life; what the child lacks in this respect, he will generally still lack as a mature person. Such is the general rule, although it is not without exceptions.

Sooner or later in the years when the child is growing to intellectual maturity, which is usually in the years following physical puberty, he experiences a crisis in which he finds himself, spiritually, forced to make a personal decision; this crisis can be summed up in the question which faced Christ's first disciples after they had known him for a short time. Christ asks them, "And what of you? Who do you say that I am?" And this question is closely connected with the other question: What do you, young man, think of yourself? Are you in your own opinion and experience someone to whom Christ has something essential to say?

The mature person encounters Christ intellectually, whereas as a child he encountered him only pictorially, in the pictures and images which touched his religious feeling. The words of the messengers who were sent out by Christ and the intellectual impression of him which they had and which they handed on to the Church of later generations, these are what face the young man in sermons and instructions as he grows to maturity.

From a psychological viewpoint, this spiritual and intellectual encounter has much in common with what has been passed on to later generations of their religious tradition by Buddha or other founders of religions, through the spiritual mediation of their disciples. Their spiritual form traverses time as a question and a call, as the image of all that is venerable. For in a transient world they proclaim the absolute. Through wise men, prophets and saints, reflections of God's mystery, the question comes, like a knocking at the door, to all men: Will you grant admittance to the Eternal One? Will you stand your ground alone or will you accept guidance from him in whom God's mystery calls? Any meeting with Christ is, however, set apart by the fact that Jesus Christ came to men as God's image and in a very different way from Buddha or Lao-tzu or Mohammed. They came only as wise teachers, as forerunners, he as God's own representative: the Son, the Mediator. "Whoever has seen me, has seen the Father" (John 14:9). None of the others spoke like this; only he could in truth say: "Come to me ... and you shall find rest for your souls" (Matt. 11: 28f.).

The confidence of faith, to which he calls men, presupposes that they are religious men, that is, men with a humble spirit towards the great God above and with love in their hearts for the Holy One; men who want to be guided in their consciences by the light "which lights all men", by the call of the eternal rather than that of temporal things, of the holy rather than the human, the all-too-human. And this sign of God, his Word in the world, speaks to the world of the love of God and of the giving up of the whole self to him. The inner "Thou shalt" indicates a spiritual order, to which man knows he owes honour and obedience.

Because of his conscience the religious man is in a strange position. If he looks at external nature and has not already gained from somewhere else intimations of a supernatural being, he sees himself confronted by a mystery as miraculous as it is terrifying. So much in nature points to an immeasurably profound and wise order and so much is enigmatic and frightening. The magnificent abundance and order of the whole is at odds with the terrible and terrifying aspect of animal nature with its pains and passions, wildness and cruelty, as though something of the awe-inspiring mythical Chaos were still at work. And if we contemplate too the history of mankind with all its riddles and the impression which man receives on considering himself, not merely speculatively and in a dream, where he sees only what in his good moments he hopes to become, but soberly and honestly as he is in reality, then we are almost inevitably reminded of the psalmist's description of man as "fearfully and wonderfully made" (Ps. 138:14). Man really is the bloom and perfection of the visible world, but seen in his historical reality and particularly in the mass, he is also something uncanny and frightening, a mixture, as Pascal pointed out, of greatness and wretchedness. He is wretched not only because of the power of evil, but also because of the social and cultural condition in which the mass of mankind vegetates to its grave with only feeble flickers of any higher aspiration, their instincts and emotions taking their course, at times accompanied by terrible excesses. And even when we consider the life of mankind in its finest forms: young men and women, splendid in their youth and growth to maturity, the hope of their parents; men of intellect and greatness of soul, the admiration of their generation – how fragile and unstable and near to nothingness is it all! If the tempest of war sweeps over nations in indiscriminating and apparently senseless destruction, if a malignant disease or an accident destroys the happiest dreams overnight – what is man then? These are the depths of the mystery in which we are immersed.

In the face of such a world, as we see it reflected both in nature and in history, any belief in God has far from insignificant difficulties for man's reason. It is not surprising that the great majority of mankind has attained no very clear picture of God, although in the depths of man's consciousness the longing, awakened by the divine Spirit, is far from dead. In nature, in history and in man's conscience, God remains hidden and "no man has ever seen God" says John (1:18). He is at work as though hidden by a veil; he has placed in the human soul intimations of greatness, in creation traces of the miraculous and in the consciousness of man a law written on the tablet of the mind, through which he speaks to man. But it is like the echo of a voice, whose source man cannot see. It is an incitement to us, as Paul says, to see "if we wish to find him". Man stands at a point of departure which is characterized by unrest, uncertainty, anxiety and yearning. To gaze out into the horrors of the world in search of the love, the intimations of which are ineradicably rooted within him – this is the highest of which man as we know him is capable. Contemplation of nature and meditation on history, a knowledge of himself and the help of his conscience can lead man, if he has the desire to follow the call of sanctity, to the threshold where he can stretch out his arms to God. Man's position in the world has been described by modern philosophers as a condition of haphazardness, of anxiety and worry, and this corresponds to the reality of the world on this side of the threshold. Some may never penetrate beyond this point and for them the darkness is permanent.

But in man there remains the yearning – St. Augustine calls it "restlessness" – and it is this deeper element in man which gives him the power to look out beyond himself. God has made him in such a way that it is precisely in the knowledge of his own hopelessness that he looks beyond himself – if not out of his own yearning, then out of that kindled in him by God's spirit. Man, as we see him in history, is not completely weighed down by sin and guilt but also upheld by the hope of salvation. In the very first chapters of man's history there shines forth the assurance: "One of your seed will crush the head of the snake." This promise belongs to the first revelation of all human history and the light which was there from the beginning before it took flesh and came as "the Light of the World", shines on every human soul.

In a talk at Notre Dame, Lacordaire,[1] drawing on Pascal as he drew on Augustine and Augustine on Paul, said: The Messianic idea was not only the animating force and determining factor in the life of the Jewish people during its pre-Christian history, but was widespread too among peoples outside Israel. All mankind, in whatever part of the world, is characterized not only by a common obscure feeling of guilt but also by the expectation of a salvation which is to come. These fears and hopes are accompanied by prayers and rites of atonement, the expression of a yearning which can only find its fulfilment through the grace which comes from above. In Christ the presentiments and prophecies of all previous eras found their fulfilment, not in any transformation of man's external condition but in the transformation of his spiritual life. This is a sign that God is at work. Men can influence both the world around them and what is to happen in the future – but what can a man do about the past? No man can choose his ancestors or arrange for himself a vanguard of prophets to prepare his way.

Now the long-awaited Saviour has come and in the areas where the Christian gospel is preached, those who

---

[1] *Œuvres* IV (1881), pp. 135ff.

are chosen learn what he said: that "here is more than all the wisdom of Solomon", that kings and wise men longed to see his day and did not see it. And the cross, the height of paradox as far as our natural feelings are concerned, "to the Jews a discouragement, to the Gentiles mere folly" when seen as the end to a holy life, towers across the centuries as a symbol of grace and the promise of eternal love.

The Word of God in Redemption

WHAT does it mean: "God speaks to man"? He spoke to
Adam, to Abraham, to Moses and the Prophets. Since he
has no body, his "word" is not the same as that of man.
He is a spirit and his spirit "fills the earth" and "we live in
him and are in him". He "speaks" to man in manifesting
himself to man, in illuminating man so that he can know
him, by "touching", "moving", or "drawing him" to
himself with his breath. He unfolds himself, reveals himself
to man and in this way gives witness of himself. St. Augustine, and after him, the Council of Orange (529) speak
of the "preparation of the inner man" by the divine
spirit's "illumination and breath of life".[1] Similarly
W. Schmidt in his study "Uroffenbarung"[2] explains God's
words in the Garden of Eden as an illumination and
impulse in the conscience, to which obedience of faith,

[1] Denzinger, *Enchiridion symbolorum . . .*, No. 177, 180.
[2] In Esser-Mausbach, *Religion, Christentum, Kirche* I (1921), pp.
481 ff.

or disobedience, corresponds on the side of man. For according to St. Thomas, a revelation is given by God even if no visible mediator is present to reveal religious understanding and it is due to God's understanding only. Consequently belief in revelation is already present when there exists in a man's soul zeal for the truth and holiness which he has seen and when he follows that light which "lights all men" (John 1:9). A man enlightened in this way, touched by this sort of inner revelation, does not need to have even an instinctive awareness or certain assurance of its divine origin. In fact he need only surrender himself to his own awakening and the idea of the holy, and follow that inner light which draws him far beyond himself, with sincere desire. This constitutes an act of faith, as was explained by theologians who have closely studied these religious problems such as Justin, Irenaeus, and Clement of Alexandria among the Fathers, then Cardinal de Lugo, Scheeben, Newman, F. Schmidt, Mausbach, Capéran, W. Schmidt, and others in more recent years.

Catholic theology assumes that God gave a general revelation or manifestation of himself to mankind, in which he spoke to men and called them all to salvation — not only man in his original state before the Fall but empirical man also. God did not leave man on his own.

The first Vatican Council distinguishes in the first place between natural and supernatural revelations[3] and goes on to emphasize the importance of God's supernatural

[3] Denzinger, *op. cit.,* No. 1785.

revelation in the following paragraph. It is owing to this revelation, the purpose of which was man's salvation, that the knowledge of God, not in itself inaccessible to the human understanding, can also in the present plight of mankind be brought to that degree of certainty and merit which is necessary for salvation.[4] But however it came about, the Fathers of the Council did certainly not want to propound a purely *natural theology* in the sense of an independent and self-sufficient system of thought, but to make clear that a real, though imperfect, knowledge of God and relationship with him is possible before and outside the Christian revelation. This is far from implying a purely rational process of perception, but on the contrary an existential answer to God's call, which involves the whole person. Therefore there is no search for God that is purely natural and separable from the redemption and its history. What men call knowledge of God, an awareness of him, is from God's point of view a revealing of himself (Rom. 1:19). Knowledge is realized in faith.[5] In an Augustinian formulation the Council of Orange teaches that no one "can think or choose rightly without the illumination or inspiration of the divine Spirit".[6] Even Karl Barth, while rejecting Emil Brunner's thesis, pays tribute to Catholic theology in that scarcely any present-day theologian ascribes to empirical mankind a true knowledge of God without preparatory or assistant

[4] Denzinger, *op. cit.,* No. 1786.
[5] G. Söhngen, *Die Einheit in der Theologie,* pp. 248 ff.
[6] Denzinger, *op. cit.,* No. 180.

grace. In other words, a natural knowledge of God, which is in itself possible, is in the actual divine plan of salvation integrated by God's supernatural revelation into the knowledge of faith. It is the Logos that "enlightens every soul" (John 1:9) and man, moved by the light of God which is given him, "believes that God exists and that he rewards those who try to find him" (Heb. 11:6).

God's general revelation presupposes on the part of fallen man a capacity to respond to God. There are in man, as St. Augustine suggested, certain outlines or traces of the original idea of God; the remains of a capacity in his feelings, in his understanding and will – or whatever names are given to the functions of the soul – through which he can answer and co-operate with God's call. By himself no one is capable of moving towards salvation;[7] any movement which is important for man's salvation is accomplished through God's gratuitous grace, the challenge of God's Word, his inspiration. But it is God's will that every man should have this sufficient grace.

Thus to speak of purely natural religion outside Christianity is justified neither theologically nor historically. From the theological viewpoint, man has no purely natural vocation or condition. From the historical viewpoint, it is common knowledge that devout men of all religions, even philosophers like Aristotle or Plato and founders of religions such as Buddha or Mohammed, as also primitive peoples or the followers of Lao-tzu or of the

[7] Denzinger, *op. cit.,* No. 811 ff.

Indian Bhagavad Gita trace their religious knowledge and experiences back to enlightenment and grace from heaven and, as Paul Claudel said of the Japanese peoples, honour "the mystery to which the heart pays homage". It is significant that the greatest of more recent religious philosophers of Catholic character, inspired alike by Bible and history of religion, such as Pascal and Newman, cannot find anything to support the idea of a natural religion. With similar aims J. Kälin O.P.[8] examines the moral values in various religious traditions and comes to the conclusion that the emotions and aspirations of the conscience are clearly penetrated by God's grace. Even Protestant theologians are beginning to adopt once again the traditionally Catholic pre-Reformation view of a general revelation for mankind's salvation. M. Lackmann[9] has already been mentioned. Wunsch[10] too, in his study on world religions and the absolutism of Christianity, shows convincingly that although cultic forms and philosophies are conditioned by locality and race, these do not affect the essence of religion, which is a relationship with God and faith as an existential attitude. The content of Christian revelation is a special gift of God; all peoples, however, participate in God's grace and God "accompanies them in his ways", not all to the same extent but giving to all what is necessary for salvation.

When fallen men are called by God's revelation, it

[8] *Rhythmen des Mondes* (1954).
[9] *Vom Geheimnis der Schöpfung,* p. 188.
[10] In the Mensching series on comparative religion.

means that they are faced with a decision: whether *excitati divina gratia et adjuti*[11] – aroused and supported by God's grace – they are to open their hearts and escape from the egocentricity which is the mark of original sin or whether they will persist in it. To a few chosen men a particular rôle in the history of man's salvation is given and they are charged with the purifying, instructing and edifying of their whole generation, often with effects which reach far into the future. The moral injunctions and cultic rites of primitive peoples as well as of highly-developed religions are derived, as they themselves believe, from divinely-inspired leaders, law-givers, priests, and prophets, all of whom are instruments of divine guidance. And even if all that is sacred is constantly threatened by human corruption, the spirit of God is always close to all men and it is due to his grace that those who are inspired by God, whatever their religious tradition, are sustained by the positive values of truth, goodness and holiness, which are found everywhere, and so as instruments of Providence become the preceptors of their brethren and of entire nations.

The election of individuals within each race corresponds to the election of Israel among the other nations. As the chosen people, Israel came relatively late on to the historical scene: with the departure of Abraham from his Chaldean home. He is the father of faith, that is of belief in God purified of all idolatrous nature worship, and it was promised him that his belief in the living God should

[11] Denzinger, *op. cit.,* No. 798.

be accompanied by the power to make mankind fruitful and that in him "all the races of the world shall find a blessing" (Gen. 12:3). The sacrificial meal as a symbol of the mysterious bond between the participants and the one supreme God is typical. The story of the sacrifice of Isaac should be interpreted as the crucial sign of a change in the story of salvation. Under the influence of the tradition which he had inherited, through which God usually makes known his will, Abraham had resolved to slay his beloved son and was at the point of doing so when it was made clear to him by God's enlightenment, in the form of an angel, that his God did not require this of him. The elevation to a higher type of theism brought with it purer rites, until the stage of bloody sacrifice of animals was overcome at the instance of the prophetic spirit and the transition was made to the spiritual "offering of praise" and to "adoration in spirit and in truth".

With Moses the faith received the strict pedagogic form of the Law and the nation was bound to a covenant with God. It cannot be denied that St. Paul from the nature of his theme in the epistle to the Romans emphasized the meaning of the Law principally from its negative side: its inability to procure salvation. Yet precisely for this reason it is the means of educating and preparing man for Christ, in that it leads him to the point where he looks out beyond his own failure in search of grace: "Pitiable creature that I am, who is to set me free from a nature thus doomed to death?" (Rom. 7:24.) Here the pedagogic importance of the Law for individuals is stressed. It was certainly far from St. Paul's intention to throw any doubt upon the fact that it had to protect the order of the community and that "the Law given through Moses" was able to raise the chosen people on theocratic authority to an exceptionally high standard of culture and morality. God's great revelation of himself preceded them in the wilderness and gave to the chosen liberator of Israel the strength of faith in the words of an eternally valid revelation: "I am who am." This has been interpreted very convincingly by Rosenzweig and Buber as: I am he who is always present wherever you are, whether you were to climb up into the highest mountain or sink into the deepest abyss, in all the sorrows and all the joys of life I am there, the stay, the prop, the demanding and yet all-merciful God, the God of your forefathers and of the Promise, far beyond the temporal pilgrimage of life: "in faith they died; for them, the promises were not fulfilled, but they looked forward to them" (Heb. 11:13).

The law as an instrument of education, codified in the precise formulae of the book of Exodus (chap. 20), covers the cultic and social life of the people and is supplemented by a liturgical arrangement of the year with its climax in the feast of the Pasch. Nonetheless, however great its originator's design, with the constant systematization introduced by Moses' successors and the strictness of its enforcement even in the smallest details of everyday life, the religion of later Judaism, when in the hands of the Pharisaic teachers of the Law, fell into the toils of human self-will and lost the free breath of life which was characteristic of the "fathers of the faith". It was against this loss that the prophets fought with passionate zeal. They

55

sought to revive the spirit of freedom and the sanctity of direct access to God. Osee, Amos, Jeremias, and the Psalms are great testimonies of religious fervour and in addition they prepare the way for the kingdom of God. To these Christ could point when he preached salvation in order to lead the people of Israel, and through them, the whole human race, to a true humanity.

"In old days, God spoke to our fathers in many ways and by many means, through the prophets; now at last in these times he has spoken to us with a Son to speak for him" (Heb. 1:1). God became flesh and through his representative speaks divine truth in the history of mankind. The incarnation of God is the miracle of God's love, eternally prophesied, and from it spring all grace, knowledge, and realization of sanctity that are or have ever been received by individuals and by nations, whether they know his name or not. In Christ is given the "fullness" of salvation, the reunion of values otherwise scattered at various levels and so the correction of all partial truths into one fulness. In the person of the eternal Word incarnate, in the man Jesus Christ "the one mediator between God and men" (1 Tim. 2:5), "the kindness of God, our Saviour, dawned on us, his great love for man" (Tit. 3:4). "There have been many prophets and kings who have longed to see what you see, and never saw it, to hear what you hear, and never heard it" (Luke 10:24). He himself is the Word and speaks the word of God in the language of human imagery, for this is the only way in which the divine mystery can be made accessible to his creatures. His life itself is the realization of what the man who is pleasing to God should be, through his complete trust in the Father and his consequent complete love of his brothers. His life demonstrates what he teaches: through him God's rule will come and he will prepare for himself a consecrated nation, as an instrument of God's rule in the world, the leaven in the mass. "He who believes", that is who follows God's call in his whole existence, will not only win salvation for himself but will also participate in Christ's mission, in God's plan of salvation for the world: "You, therefore, must go out, making disciples of all nations" (Matt. 28:19).

The preaching of the apostles whom he sent out as his witnesses, the Holy Scripture of the New Testament which sprang from the apostolic proclamation, the Church's service of the Word with the sacramental signs of grace, the solemn decisions of the whole Church, through its teaching authority, by which it preserves the one and only Revelation of Christ – these are the means, which the Word of God uses so that the kingdom of God which came with Christ may have its witnesses throughout the future. "God speaks to men through men."[12] "Who hears you, hears me." Outwardly his call comes through men, inwardly and simultaneously he calls men through the Holy Spirit, who enlightens their hearts. So faith is not merely a matter of holding that certain past events of our salvation are true – even though this is the basis of all further preaching of the Word. The meaning and purpose of all God's communication with men through the ages is

---

[12] Augustine, *On Christian Doctrine*, prol. 5–6.

always the formation of an immediate personal relationship between God and the individual and all mediation aims to develop this. The whole mission of the Church rests on one thing: service to the kingdom of God, so that the relationship between God and man, represented in Christ, can be realized from generation to generation and Christ continues his life in a people who are sanctified. Each individual is approached for his free decision. God's call corresponds to man's obedience in faith. From the first movement of salvation to the final perfection of the individual, there is ever present the mystery of the communication and interplay of God's operation on man and man's free response to God.

How does the Church proclaim the word of God? If this question was put to the ordinary believer, the man in the street, the answer would doubtless refer you – apart from religious instruction for children – to the Sunday sermon, probably with a more or less critical comment. And it cannot be denied that in this respect, as a proclamation of the word of God, the average sermon lags far behind the homilies of the Fathers of the Church. The same is still partly true, and was completely true until the liturgical revival of recent times, of many popular books of edification, including prayer-books and hymn-books in common use. In comparison with the texts of adoration, thanksgiving, repentance, humility, hope and love to be found in Holy Scripture, the impression given by these books is at times far from edifying. L. Agustoni expresses this positively when he says, "We should offer God's people the bread of the word of God in a worthy fashion as

58

regards both language and content, and not betray God's word by making digressions in the form of all sorts of foreign-sounding clauses."[13]

Nonetheless, it is one-sided to think only of the sermon when speaking of the preaching of God's word. For it is to neglect something both important and consoling: all that the liturgy of the Church means and has always meant as advocate of the word in the life of the Church. Catholics believe that Christ remains ever-present to his faithful people through word and sacrament; and in the cultic mystery of the liturgy these two are bound together in an inner unity. The liturgy is a sacramental act, accompanied by God's word, the purpose of which is to enable man's faith to comprehend the operation of salvation and the imparting of Christ through the Holy Spirit. The word of God belongs to the act of worship and lends to the rite its meaning and richness in merit.

We are accustomed to think of Christ giving himself above all in Communion and so imperceptibly – probably in reaction against the one-sided emphasis given to the word of God in Protestantism – the efficacious power of the divine word has been under-estimated. The liturgy of the Church, however, has objectively remained unaffected by this. It is far more than a pious pretence that the Church bases her *sacrificium laudis,* her sacrifice of praise offered in association with Christ, especially on Holy Scripture. It can be seen as one of God's miracles in the Church that through the ages the liturgy in a very special

[13] "Das Wort Gottes als kultisches Wort" in *Anima* (1955, Sept.).

way has translated and translates God's word into actual terms. The word of the Scripture and the sacramental rite co-operate in the mystery of the cultic act.

"The Church is not only the Church of the Word (the tendency of Protestantism) and not only the Church of the Sacraments (the tendency of the Eastern Church) but the Church both of the Word and of the Sacrament."[14] Nonetheless, it must be emphasized that this is no more than a "tendency" or "danger" of the Protestant or of the Eastern way of thought. Many attempts are being made to overcome this one-sidedness. For example, H. Vogel[15] writes: "God's revelation of himself is a revelation of the Word in which God reveals himself as his own advocate" and "God's revelation of himself is a revelation of action in that the Creator and Redeemer as an active force manifests himself in his omnipotence and mercy." And another writer says:[16] "In every word which is spoken in Christ lives the Word which is Christ himself." "For thy word, my Lord and God, is the light of my soul and the holy sacrament is the bread of my life."[17] If the sacrament takes effect *ex opere operato,* that is, of itself, through the action of Christ, it only does so in relation to faith, the *opus operantis.* The Word of God makes it possible for faith to appreciate the work of our redemption; it is God's gift for the nourishment of faith "something alive, full of energy" (Heb. 4:12); it pene-

---

[14] Schmaus, *Katholische Dogmatik* IV/1 (1952), p. 26.
[15] *Gott in Christo* (1951), pp. 173, 178.
[16] H. Kuhaupt, *Die Feier der Eucharistie* II (1951), p. 54.
[17] *Imitation of Christ* IV, 11.

60

trates the soul and "you recognize it for what it is, God's message" (1 Thess. 2:13); you must "cherish that word implanted in you which can bring salvation to your souls" (Jas. 1:21); it "has its uses; to instruct us, to expose our errors, to correct our faults, to educate us in holy living" (2 Tim. 3:16). As L. Agustoni says, "In this respect we must recognize fully the truth that the Protestant liturgy possesses in its teaching, in its estimation of God's word: it is penetrated by the belief in Christ's presence in the word of worship – the error lies in its exclusiveness",[18] in the fact that the sacramental aspect is pushed out by the word, a loss which has been felt by many Protestants in recent years and which they are trying to overcome. As well as W. Stählin and H. Asmussen among others, H. Vogel can once again be cited in support: "The sacraments which are constituted of both word and element are not only signs or symbols, but instruments of the Lord who is acting on our behalf in them and through them and giving himself to us.... Baptism is the consecration to redemption and cannot be separated from faith – it is in this way that God gives us the beginning of our affiliation to Christ. The grace of God which precedes all our faith, hope and charity initiates us into life with Christ through baptism. The starting-point for us will not be the experience of conversion or the encounter with faith as such, but that basic preparatory grace which is given to us in the beginning by baptism. This is of importance as far as the baptism of children is concerned, in that it

---

[18] Agustoni, *op. cit.;* cf. Denzinger, *op. cit.,* No. 847–51.

particularly stresses the prevenient character of baptismal grace."

The thought of Holy Scripture and the teaching of the Church consider divine causality, the power of the Holy Spirit in salvation, on the one hand as the effecting or deepening, by the Holy Spirit, of man's membership of the Body of Christ through the sacramental sign: "Be baptized, every one of you, in the name of Jesus Christ, to have your sins forgiven" (Acts 2:38)[19] and on the other hand as his awakening of the disposition of faith necessary for salvation. Baptism is "the sacrament of faith"[20] and all the sacraments are, according to Thomas, "the signs by which faith can be recognized" *(signa protestantia fidem)*, the faith through which man is justified. "The sacrament is brought about by the joining together of the word of faith which we proclaim and the element."[21] Therefore either the sacrament alone can be stressed – which would favour its misunderstanding as magical – or faith alone. The latter would imply a return to the Messalian doctrine of enthusiasm, exemplified in the "Spiritual Homilies" of Macarius Magnus (about 400 A.D.) who was attacked by many of the Fathers[22] and condemned in 390 at the Synod of Side and again in 431

---

[19] Cf. John 3:5; Rom. 6:3ff.; Tit. 3:5; Denzinger, *op. cit.,* No. 799, 847; Thomas, *Summa theol.* III, 62, 1 and 6; Schmaus, *Dogmatik* III/2 (1941), pp. 41ff.

[20] Council of Trent: Denzinger, *op. cit.,* No. 799.

[21] Augustine, *In Joh. Ev.* 80, 3.

[22] Particularly Diadochus of Photike, Chapters on spiritual perfection: *Migne* PG 45, 1167ff.

at the Council of Ephesus.[23] Nevertheless these ideas were revived in the sixteenth century.[24]

If, however, the Catholic doctrine of the parity and unity of faith and sacraments were to be reaffirmed, it would really only be a question of guarding against too great a bias in either direction. It would then be possible either to side with the Fathers of the Church and the Tridentine theologians in stressing the efficacy of the sacrament, with faith a necessary prerequisite, and opposing any restriction of the action of the Spirit to mystical experience (Messalian and modernist heresies) or to the word of faith (the older Protestant view); or else to sympathize with Protestant philosophy in stressing faith alone, for fear of a primitive misunderstanding of the *opus operatum* as something magical, and explaining the sacrament as an efficacious sign for arousing faith. If these conditions were fulfilled, the various different emphases could be regarded as legitimate variants of the same belief within the Church.

[23] See F. Dörr, *Diadochus of Photike* (1937), pp. 11 f. For the Messalian degradation of the Sacraments, see ibid., pp. 45 ff.
[24] Denzinger, *op. cit.*, No. 847 ff.

The Ministry of the Church:
Concept and History

With Christ came the promised kingdom of the "Son of Man", "the people set apart for the most High"; the Church of Christ as an historical body for all time, as a community of "all those who believe in his name" (John 1:12), became reality. "Apostles and prophets are the foundation" on which the Church is built (Eph. 2:20). It is composed of men, of whom each one is called by faith to be a witness for the kingdom of God. The faith of the people of God is not without what St. Thomas called "the order of love" as well as an hierarchical order; the apostolic office and the witness to Christ shown by the faithful condition one another.

Jesus gave the apostles their mission and authority with the promise of his help and support for all time. The Orthodox Church, the Church of England and the Roman Catholic Church are in agreement as far as the apostolic succession is concerned, although Protestant influences within Anglicanism have resulted in a discrepancy between the substance and the theological esti-

64

mation of the episcopal powers. Basically, however, as Bishop Newbigin says, there would be no continuous following of generations in contact with Christ without the permanent office derived from the apostles; for the relationship of the individual to Christ should not be interpreted individualistically; it is based on membership of the Body of Christ, which is a visible, social, organic whole, inspired by the Spirit of Christ and therefore "the Church cannot live except as a visible defined and organized body with a continuing structure".[1]

At the time of the German Reformation the Augsburg Confession[2] declared a pastoral ministry to be necessary to the Church by divine ordinance. This was an attempt to keep open a link with the old Church. The bishops were to be retained only if they were "true bishops" in the spirit of the gospel; if they failed, emergency powers could be invoked to appoint pastors. However, as W. Stählin says:[3] "What is meaningful and, in exceptional cases, perhaps practicable as an emergency measure, must, when put forward as a theological principle, destroy not only the office, but the community too." H. Vogel[4] admits that the Augsburg article which defines the Church as "the communion of believers in Jesus Christ united in word and sacrament" does not really answer the question as to "the form of the Church, which lives from justification in Jesus Christ" and the whole history of Protestantism is

[1] Lesslie Newbigin, *The Household of God* (1953), p. 72.
[2] Art. 38.
[3] *Vom göttlichen Geheimnis* (1936).
[4] *Gott in Christo* (1951), p. 54.

"an indication of the fact that the question of the Church as such is still in need of a solution". In his principal work[5] Calvin recognizes the ministry of the Church as an apostolic foundation and sees in it a guarantee of "the immutable character of the Church"; since, however, in the late Middle Ages the apostolic succession had been degraded to a mechanical handing-on of authority and had become estranged from the spirit of the Bible, the "elders" had to consecrate elders and as "preachers" the pastors were responsible for the proclamation of the gospel. Without doubt this limitation of the functions of ministry to the service of the word and the tendency to affirm that each community was self-sufficient in the Holy Spirit, favoured a development in the direction of a secularized idea of the ministry at the time of the Enlightenment. At all events, there are indications here too that a new conception of the official priesthood is developing.

The Catholic doctrine of the Church and her ministries is derived from the incarnation of the invisible God in Jesus Christ, which revealed an historical reality for all time. The Church as the Body of Christ has received from her Head through the ages the grace and the mission to transmit the work of salvation to succeeding generations. The agents responsible for this mediation, from the time of the apostles, are the shepherds of the Church through the ages. Their authority and direction, which cannot be separated from love and which always work in fraternal affection with the faithful, as well as with authority in the

[5] *Institutions* IV, 3–4.

name of Christ, have to protect Revelation from human-ization and schisms, in order to impart to the people of the time the saving powers of Christ in word and in sacrament and to "actualize" them (as Daniélou[6] puts it) for the changing needs of the time.

Opinions on the justification for, and necessity of, the sacred office vary in modern Protestantism. Every conceivable view is found from, for instance, Emil Brunner's idea of a purely charismatic Church of "brotherliness", which is also current among American sects, to the liturgically influenced episcopal church envisaged by the group of Berneuchen theologians or by Friedrich Heiler. A more moderate line is adopted by Lutherans such as Heinrich von Campenhausen in his book on the pastoral office and priestly authority in the first three centuries[7] and the ecumenically-minded New Testament theologian Oscar Cullmann, in a number of important studies.[8] The main problem for them and even more for the others is whether and in what sense a spiritual ministry in the Church has permanent validity. Heinrich von Campenhausen definite-ly acknowledges that, by virtue of the apostolic institu-tion, there were in the early Church authoritative powers which were handed on – that is, in the Judæo-Christian branch descended from the first apostles. It was, in his view, the peculiarity of the Judæo-Christian type of

---

[6] *Le mystère de l'histoire* (1953); cf. Pius XII, *Mystici Corporis*.

[7] *Kirchliches Amt und geistliche Vollmacht in den ersten drei Jahr-hunderten* (1953).

[8] Including *Peter: Disciple – Apostle Martyr* (1953); *Christ and Time* (1962).

67

community to trace the spiritual function of the "elders" back to the apostolic laying-on of hands. He maintains, however, that, parallel to this, in the Hellenic world under the direction of the apostle Paul, and thus equally under apostolic authority, a "charismatic type of Church" developed in which the principal idea was of different offices and gifts of the Spirit which "are not in themselves capable of being handed on but are always a direct gift of the Spirit".[9] Therefore, according to the original Pauline teaching, there could be no handing-on of powers through men: "The man called by the Spirit knew himself to be called to office and the question of how presbyters and leading personalities attained their office cannot be asked in view of the significance of such powers. Indeed, the question is entirely superfluous." This is a variant of the widespread Protestant view according to which the form of the office is purely a question of expediency and not of divine right.

We must consider whether the pure charismatic of the Pauline communities has in fact any biblical foundation. Any such affirmation presupposes that in the apostolic Church there were two opposing systems, the Judæo-Christian, derived from the first apostles, and the Pauline charismata. But how then would the apostolic "pillars" have been able to "join their right hands in fellowship" with Paul (Gal. 2:9)? "There can be no question of two early communities and two separate concepts of the Church."[10] And the absolute charismatic concept is not in accord

[9] H. von Campenhausen, *op. cit.,* note 7.
[10] A. Oepke, *Das neue Gottesvolk* (1950).

with facts testified by the Bible, such as the invocation of
the Spirit for the handing-on of the powers through men.[11]
The rôle of the Spirit is neither excluded nor made superfluous by messengers, as it is not by the sacramental sign
generally; rather it is the Spirit who is the real source of the
mission. The apostle, the man, is but the instrument acting
in the name of the Spirit; the act of faith on the part of the
recipient is presupposed as a condition of the validity of
the consecration.

In his study of the Christian community in the New
Testament,[12] in which he compares the gospels (the early
apostolic tradition) with St. Paul, Eduard Schweizer also
reached the conclusion that there were two kinds of
Church, one led by the hierarchy, the other purely
charismatic with the community participating freely. Let
us try to follow his arguments:

> 1. "Paul (1 Cor. 12) recognizes only charismatic func-
> tions." – But are not 1 Thessalonians 5:12; Philippians
> 1:1; Hebrews 13:17 with their admonitions of obe-
> dience to responsible superiors not Pauline too? And
> what of the statements in Acts 14:23 and 20:17 ff.
> concerning the consecration and appointment of
> responsible presbyters in the Pauline communities?

> 2. "In 1 Corinthians 12 'apostles, prophets and
> teachers' seem indeed to take precedence, but the
> whole context of chapters 12–14 stresses the funda-

---

[11] Acts 6:6; 13:1f.; 20:28; 2 Tim. 1:6f., 14.
[12] *Die Gemeinde nach dem Neuen Testament* (1949).

mental equality of all positions." – Certainly equality is stressed in so far as all are there for the sake of the community and through the one Spirit, but it is clearly stated that they have not all the same duties: "Are all of us apostles, all prophets, all teachers?" And are charismatic gifts in some way incompatible with the duties of an official position? Are they not rather the best recommendation for candidates for ecclesiastical office?

3. "When reading the gospels we are forced to ask ourselves whether in the first Christian community there was not a completely different concept of the Church than that which we find in 1 Corinthians 12–14, for instance." This would imply that "in a certain sense the post-Pauline community (with its hierarchical character) developed, without reference to St. Paul, direct from the early communities which existed previous to or concurrently with the Pauline ones." – Such a construction is quite impossible in face of the Pauline texts already mentioned in the objections to 1 and when the reference in Galatians 2:9 to Paul's working with the original apostles is taken into account.

4. "Throughout the expression 'office' (*leiturgia*) is avoided and 'service' (*diakonia*) substituted." Later, however, we find a note to the effect that "it is precisely Paul himself who provides the only exception to this rule in Romans 15:16 and Philippians 2:17". – This surely suggests that Paul uses both terms interchangeably and with the same meaning, because the

word "office" has not the sense of personal power but of service for the Church, which is inspired by love.

5. "Apart from the historically unique position of the apostles there is neither in Paul nor in the whole New Testament any service which could not, on principle be carried out by all rather than one special person alone. It is true that in 1 Thessalonians 5:12 reference is made to 'those who have charge over you in the Lord and give you directions', but in v. 14 the whole community is exhorted to the same duties as are given to them." – It is precisely this balance between communal witness and qualified authority, between the priesthood of all believers and the special priesthood, between the general and the particular responsibility for Church discipline, which is essential to the Catholic idea of the Church and to which early Christian literature testifies.

Nonetheless, it would be unfair to theologians like von Campenhausen to see them fundamentally as opponents of the idea of an ecclesiastical office. Basically the theory of the "Pauline" charismata is only intended to counteract an "ever-threatening" excess of clerical authority with its consequent "rejection and suppression on principle of the free gifts of the Spirit".[13] This is the reason for von Campenhausen's opposition of the "ideal church" of charismatic love to the hierarchical church and he makes it clear that this is a matter of, as it were, an "utopian"

[13] H. von Campenhausen, *op. cit.*, p. 328.

attempt on the part of St. Paul, which soon lost its *raison d'être* on account of the inevitable tightening of ecclesiastical control in the struggle with Gnosticism.[14] "The real difficulty, which is always encountered, lies in deciding the proper relationship between the official hierarchy and spiritual authority." Spirit and office "have their origin in Christ and serve his will – in face of these primal truths in the life of the Church, a particular office or special gifts of the Spirit are fundamentally subordinate ideas".[15] Thus it is easy to see that the criticism is basically directed against a "mechanical" handing-on of authority and naturally and rightly lays emphasis on the spirit of the hierarchy and not merely on the form of the institution. H. Vogel, too, explains the apostolic succession in the sense that each holder of the office "gives himself the power and can hand it on to others ... as though transmitting by magic an actual possession" (*Gott in Christo*, p. 898). Neither is true since, first, all spiritual power, although truly received, is but a function of love as far as Christ and the Church are concerned[16]; secondly, there is no question of "magical" or "mechanical" handing-on of authority, as we intend to show.

The misgivings about a "mechanical" handing-on of authority rest on misapprehensions. E. Stauffer[17] and E. Kohlmeyer[18] have given historical proofs that, as far as the

[14] *Op. cit.,* pp. 69, 328.
[15] *Op. cit.,* p. 324.
[16] Cf. W. Soloviev in *Irenikon* (1926), p. 74; O. Karrer, *Peter and the Church* (1963), p. 136.
[17] *Zeitschrift für Religions- und Geistesgeschichte* (1952), pp. 207 ff.
[18] *Zeitschrift für Rechtsgeschichte* (1952), Kan. Abt. p. 1.

lists of succession of bearers of office are concerned, they were taken over from ancient Jewish traditions and were not an innovation of anti-Gnostic churchmen in the second century. These misgivings, however, are above all due to a theological misunderstanding of the idea of "apostolic succession" and J. P. Michael[19] rightly points out how important it is for the ecumenical exchange of views in recent discussions on the apostolic succession that it should be made quite clear what is meant by consecration as the handing-on of spiritual authority.

It must be observed from the outset that the apostolic succession is not bound up with the evidence of unbroken succession lists of bishops. For even if normally the individual bishop can, with as much certainty as is humanly possible, claim the validity of the consecration of his "spiritual forefathers" through the centuries, no one would make certainty about it dependent upon proof for every link in the chain. It is sufficient to know that the succession in office, emphasized by the solemnity of consecration and investiture, was at all times administered publicly and was as official as was the Church herself. Supposing, however, there were serious doubts about one of these links, say in the ninth century, concerning the intention in which consecration was administered to a "spiritual son"[20] would the whole chain be endangered? But this would be a misinterpretation of consecration, regarding it merely as endowed with human and causal continuity, as though it

[19] *Der heilige Bonifatius und die Frage der apostolischen Sukzession* (1954), p. 38.
[20] Cf. J. Scheeben, *Dogmatik* I, n. 82 and 110–15.

were a sort of "inheritance" passed from the consecrator to the consecrated. Yet it is the Holy Spirit, the "soul of the universal Church", as the early Fathers call him, who consecrates. The Church as the communion of saints, the "bride" of Christ in the Holy Spirit and the bearer of the powers of salvation, is the life-giving "mother" in all sacraments, whereas the occupants of office are only "middlemen" or agents, as Augustine suggested in his dispute with the Donatists.[21] Only the whole Church in the Holy Spirit "inspired herself by the Spirit, possesses the power to produce new life from the Spirit ... 'It is not even the saints who bring this about, but the Holy Spirit working through them' (Augustine)."[22] The handing-on of spiritual authority depends, therefore, less on the historical chain of chronologically successive acts of consecration than on the efficacious presence of Christ, the risen Lord, through the Spirit which he promised us. The motive power comes not so much from the past, from the horizontal plane, as it were, however indisputably necessary this may be, as from the vertical dimension of the Spirit ever-present through time and space, from the inner depths of the Church herself, which is his "temple" (1 Cor. 3:16). At the consecration the occupant of the office is, as it were, the impersonal medium, whom God is using for bestowing his grace. Personally an unworthy man he has no link with the imparting of this grace, but the mark of

[21] Friedrich Hofmann, *Der Kirchenbegriff des hl. Augustin* (1933), p. 257; cf. B. Poschmann, *Penance and the Anointing of the Sick* (1963) and J. Mausbach, *Ethik des hl. Augustin* II, pp. 328, 352.
[22] F. Hofmann, *op. cit.,* p. 266.

consecration enables him to make those visible signs in which the power of God is at work.[23]

The temporal chain of succession is, therefore, merely the human side of the mystery. It is not like a relay race in which the baton is passed from hand to hand. The continuity comes from an invisible sphere, not from men but through them, whether they are gold, silver or clay vessels.[24] Newman drew on the Catholic tradition to express this truth while he was still a member of the Church of England: "We call his presence in this Holy Sacrament a spiritual presence . . . by way of expressing that he who is present there can neither be seen nor heard; that he cannot be approached or ascertained by any of the senses; that he is not present in place, that he is not present carnally, though he is really present. And how this is, of course, is a mystery. All that we know or need know is that he *is* given to us . . . . The Sacraments are instruments of the application of his merits to individual believers. Though he now sits on the right hand of God, he has in one sense never left the world since he first entered it; for, by the ministration of the Holy Ghost, he is really present with us in an unknown way, and ever imparts himself to those who seek him. Even when visibly on earth he, the Son of Man, was still 'in heaven' and now, though he is ascended on high, he is still on earth. And as he is still with us, for all that he is in heaven, so, again, is the hour of his cross and passion ever mystically present . . . . Time and space have no

---

[23] *Op. cit.,* p. 415.
[24] St. Augustine, *C. ep. Parm.* 2, II, 24.

portion in the spiritual kingdom which he has founded;
and the rites of his Church are as mysterious spells by which
he annuls them both .... Thus Christ shines through them,
as through transparent bodies, without impediment. He is
the Light and Life of the Church, acting through it,
dispensing of his fulness, knitting and compacting together
every part of it .... Just as it is not man but Christ who
baptizes (1 Cor. 12:13), although in the temporal, visible
sphere man is the minister of baptism, so it is Christ and
not man who consecrates, although in the temporal visible
sphere man is the instrument of consecration: Christ has
breathed on men and given them his Spirit to help them
in their mission .... The grace given to the people of the
New Testament is to see Christ in all things, revealed under
a visible sign; to meditate on his channels of grace, not for
themselves, but as symbols of his presence and power."[25]

We now come to the actual proofs for the "apostolic
succession". The term does not mean that the apostolic
office as such (that is, the direct commissioning of the
eye-witnesses of Christ) is continued – for "the bishops
are truly the successors of the apostles without themselves
being apostles, the Pope is truly the successor of Peter
without himself being one of the first apostles."[26] It means
that there is a continuity in authority from the apostles
to the bishops which is translated into real terms by the
Spirit through the sacramental laying-on of hands. In this
sacrament is bestowed the spiritual power to preserve the

[25] Newman, *Parochial and Sermons* VI, 11 and III, 19.
[26] G. Söhngen, *Die Einheit in der Theologie* (1952), p. 307.

benefits of salvation divinely revealed to the apostles, more precisely to continue the threefold ministry of Christ in the body of the Church: the teaching ministry in the responsible proclamation of the gospel, the priestly ministry in administering of the sacraments, the kingly ministry of Christ in guiding the faithful so that the unity of the Church is preserved. This connection of authority has biblical grounds: Christ gave to the apostles, and so indirectly to those whom they consecrated and to whom they handed on their authority until the end of time, the power of binding and loosing in his name: "I promise you, that all you bind on earth shall be bound in heaven, and all that you loose on earth shall be loosed in heaven" (Matt. 18:18) and "All authority in heaven and earth, he said, has been given to me; you, therefore, must go out, making disciples of all nations . . . . And behold I am with you through all the days that are coming, until the consummation of the world" (Matt. 28:18–20).

These solemn words of promise and of authority applied first and foremost to the apostles, but not only in a personal sense, for the apostles will not be there "through all the days". The words applied to them as holders of Christ's authority whose task is to proclaim the gospel, to baptize and to instruct all nations in the spirit of Christ. It is Christ's will that there should always be bearers of this apostolic authority, that the apostles should have successors to their task until the end of time. Naturally all those who, by virtue of the "royal priesthood of all believers", preserve a continuity with the first apostles, all those who "are to find faith in me through their word" (John 18:20),

77

share to a certain extent in the promise and in the authority.

The principle of succession in responsible service of the community was familiar from the Old Testament, for "it played an important rôle in the ancient biblical world":[27] the office of mediator, which Moses received from the hand of God, is unique, yet he appointed Josue as his successor (Num. 27:18ff.). The teachers of Israel, as Our Lord himself recognized, sit in "the chair of Moses" (Matt. 23:2). The apostles came from this world and adapted the basic ideas of the older people of God in a Christian sense to the organization of the Church. Various studies[28] show that the conclusion of recent research on the subject is that "before early Christianity entered the Hellenic world, its fundamental concepts had been formed by its native soil in Jewish Palestine".[29] In the same way that the Christian service has grown out of the Jewish – the inheritance of the synagogue being enriched by the christological idea – so the binding and loosing – used in Rabbinical terminology for spiritual powers in the community – and also the laying-on of hands as a sign of the handing-on of authority are adumbrated in the Old Testament (Num. 8:10f.; 27:18).

Or was it Jesus' intention, as Protestant theologians generally hold, to institute an apostolic office in his name only for the beginning, at least in so far as all later ecclesiastical offices could not any more appeal to a "divine

[27] E. Stauffer, *Theologie des Neuen Testamentes* (1948), pp. 215f.

[28] Particularly those of G. Dalman, A. Schlatter, R. Bultmann, G. Kittel, F. C. Grant.

[29] G. Kittel, *Die Probleme des paläst. Spätjudentums* (1926), p. 2.

right" but would have to be formed according to the discretion of the Church. Using this argument Oscar Cullmann believes that the apostolic succession can be demolished on the grounds of the biblical concept of time. He argues that the history of redemption had its "unique focal point" at the time of the apostolic institution and that this age is the "guiding principle and norm" for all subsequent ages. It is the "time of direct revelation or of the Incarnation" that ended with the death of the last apostolic eye-witness.[30] The post-apostolic time is cognate with the time of Our Lord and possesses its own value; for the life and death of Christ are continued by the Church and we are now in the "time of salvation". Nonetheless, apostles and bishops are "on quite different levels"; and the members of the Church in the ages after the apostles are characterized by the fact that they believe "through their word (John 17:20), that is, through the Scriptures" which were collected together in the canon of the New Testament about 150 A.D. and to which apostolic authority was extended through the Holy Spirit.[31] Consequently the apostolic office continues to operate only in the "apostolic writings" and all ecclesiastical exegeses which claim to be "infallible guides" inevitably tend towards a devaluation of the testimony of Revelation.

By way of digression, we should like to observe that some Protestant theologians affirm, as though it were a kind of catchword, that the Church is not based on the

---

[30] Denzinger, *Enchiridion symbolorum . . .*, No. 2021.
[31] O. Cullmann, *Tradition* (1954), pp. 29–33, 44–48.

apostolic succession of office but on the apostolic succession of creed, that is on nothing more than biblical faith, in so far as the individual Christian or official minister "serves the same word of whom the apostles were witnesses".[32] Similarly H. Asmussen, speaking for all the theologians of the Synod of Barmen, writes: "The holders of office are successors of the apostles only in the same sense as every member of the community. The Church is apostolic because God's word, given to us in the apostolic message, is alive in her. No magic or mystical powers are procured by the prayers and laying-on of hands at ordination; the laying-on of hands is an outward sign that a mission and a privilege is being bestowed on a particular man . . . . The form in which the Church is to be governed is not laid down in the gospels; to decide it is the task of the community (Church), but the community is not justified in letting the matter go out of its control."[33] Quite apart from the misunderstanding indicated in the use of the word "magic", many of these theologians felt in fact obliged to restrict this presumed ability of the Church to regulate her own hierarchical structure, in the knowledge that the New Testament, and thus the early Church, in the Acts of the Apostles and in the epistles only knew and recognized one sort of legitimate handing-on of office established by the apostles. It must also not be overlooked that without the apostolically appointed bearers of office (in the authority of their succession through the laying-on of

[32] H. Vogel, *Gott in Christo,* p. 898.
[33] *Consensus de doctrina Evangelii* (1937), pp. 200f.

hands in the Holy Spirit) neither the *regula fidei* (the creed) nor the canon of Scripture would have come into existence. W. Elert[34] is close to the truth when he argues that episcopal office (in the apostolic succession), creed and canon of Scripture must be considered jointly. The uniform faith, which through joint episcopal action found its expression in the common Creed and the common canon of Scripture, was the prerequisite for the common participation in the Eucharistic act of worship. This Eucharistic participation in its turn was controlled by the bishops' discipline of penance – and new arrivals carried letters of credence from their previous episcopal see, so that uniformity of faith and the uniform nature of the community of saints would be guaranteed. Ultimately everything depended thus on the leadership of the Church through the continuing unity of the holders of episcopal office.

It is true that the apostolic office as such was unique, that the preaching of the apostles is the foundation stone for all following ages and that no new revelations can "enlarge upon" that given by Christ.[35] The holders of authority in the Church after the time of its foundation "occupy their position of authority on trust as it were from the apostles."[36] But by the power of the promised Spirit, who is given to the Church for ever, they share in the infallibility of the universal Church in so far as they represent the Church united under the Petrine office. The function of the post-

[34] *Abendmahl und Kirchengemeinschaft in der alten Kirche* (1955).
[35] Denzinger, *op. cit.,* No. 2021.
[36] W. Mundle in *Zeitschrift für neutestamentliche Wissenschaft* (1928), p. 40.

apostolic teaching office as regards Revelation is thus "not constitutive but directive",[37] in contrast with the mission of the apostles. Its task is to apply the faith to the problems of any and every age and to preserve at the same time the apostolic tradition: not to create new revelations. In her early years the Church was concerned first to ensure Christian freedom in opposition to the Jewish following of the law, then to protect the apostolic tradition against the Gnostic secret cults, and also to define the canon of Scripture in the face of the apocryphal versions then spreading like wildfire and to formulate the true doctrine of the Trinity and the Incarnation as against Arian rationalism. In the whole post-apostolic era the Church's task is rather to preach to all generations the good news she has received. To help her in this task under the sacred ministry, she has been promised the constant presence of Christ "all through the days that are coming, until the consummation of the world" (Matt. 28:20).

From a religious point of view it is completely unimportant whether our conception of time is cyclic as was that of the Greeks or linear like that of the Jews. The Bible is not dealing with time merely in a terrestrial and astronomical sense; faith is not bound up with any scientific view of the world. To be a Christian we are obliged to believe neither that the earth is the centre of the universe nor that the Jewish view of time as a continuous line is correct. The sole determining factor biblically is the continuing presence of the risen Lord through his Spirit, "the saving presence

[37] J. Daniélou in *Dieu vivant* (1953), pp. 17 ff.

of God efficacious in faith".[38] What is of significance where our redemption is concerned is "not the constant movement of time but the confrontation of man with Christ, that is with God".[39] When John's writings are examined, it can be seen that the New Testament cannot be reduced simply to the concept of time as a continuing line; the spiritual presence of Christ in the communion of saints, in the preaching of the word and in the sacramental worship of the community breaks into the line of earthly time, "the future aeon becoming actuality".[40] In this way, the ancient Jewish linear time, which looked to a salvation always in the future, is overcome: the faithful are face to face with Christ: "Maran atha" – the Lord is here.

Oscar Cullmann presumes that it is through Scripture (and through Scripture alone) that the apostolic authority continues to operate and so he is able both to establish the authority of Scripture and make a distinction between it and the tradition of the Church. The Catholic Church too, however, professes that Revelation, through the tradition received from the apostles, "from the Lord" (1 Cor. 11:23), is enshrined in the testimony of the New Testament writings. And we are free, with Newman, Dubarle, Geiselmann and other Catholic theologians, to examine closely the Tridentine decrees and conclude that one possible interpretation of the pronouncement on "Holy Scripture and the apostolic tradition" in the fourth session

[38] J. Körner (following Bultmann) in *Ev. Theologie* (1954), pp. 177 ff.
[39] W. G. Kümmel, *Verheißung und Erfüllung* (1945), p. 95.
[40] J. Schniewind, *Messiasgeheimnis und Eschatologie* (1952), p. 10.

is that the whole apostolic preaching of the gospel (in all that is necessary for salvation) is included in the scriptures of the New Testament and that the Scriptures therefore do contain the whole Revelation for the post-apostolic generations and are the source, the final foundation and the *norma normans* of Christian belief. It is thus possible to say with even greater assurance that the post-apostolic tradition is "only" (but indispensably) important in so far as it has the task of "infallibly preserving and faithfully interpreting"[41] Revelation under the guidance of the teaching office of the Church. In supposing the one and only intervention of the infallible divine Spirit with divine and apostolic authority in the post-apostolic era to have taken place when the canon of Scripture was established around 150 A.D., Cullmann is giving a far from adequate explanation of the facts. It was in 150 that, under the impact of a shortening of the Bible by Marcion and of Gnostic fabrications, the bishops realized the necessity of collecting the apostolic writings as an authoritative standard. But this collection is clearly seen to be the work of the Spirit throughout a whole series of generations. Indeed, under the direction of the major episcopal sees and ultimately of the Roman seat of Peter the process of delimitation as regards other "works of edification" and apocryphal writings, was carried out in subsequent centuries and concluded in the fourth. It is, therefore, impossible to speak of a single intervention and guidance of the Holy Spirit (which would leave the canon in the air, so to speak) but rather the support

[41] I. *Conc. Vat.* 4, 4.

of the Spirit applies equally to all the period of time and, moreover, to the preservation of the apostolic witness throughout the whole post-apostolic tradition. To assume that there was any special intervention of the infallible Spirit in the compilation of the canon or in the continuing preservation of apostolic witness seems to us completely unnecessary. For as far as the compilation of the canon was concerned it was only a matter of laying down, by means of the normal working of the Church in the Holy Spirit, what the testimonies of the Christian community, already there from the beginning and handed on, said about their apostolic origin, that is about the authors of the Scriptures used by the Church. The inspired nature of these writings and their providential significance as authentic testimony of the beliefs of the apostles had already been accepted quite independently of their subsequent recognition by later ages of the Church. These later ages had nothing original to add; their task was to preserve and protect against distortions all that already existed from apostolic times.

If it is thought that the compilation of the canon, the collection of the true apostolic writings, was suggested to the Church "purely by her inner apostolic authority, just as it still is today, because Christ the Kyrios speaks in her",[42] then it would be historically more accurate to say with Harnack that it was "because this procedure met with universal acceptance on its own merits backed by the authority of the Roman Church", that the other

---

[42] O. Cullmann, *Tradition,* p. 47.

provinces of the Church subscribed to the Roman canon.[43] Or was perhaps "the inner apostolic authority" sufficient to obtrude of itself on those early Christian communities and devout people, who also considered the *Shepherd of Hermas,* the *Teaching of the Twelve Apostles,* the first and second Letters of Clement and that of Barnabas as "apostolic and inspired"? Surely the "inner apostolic authority" shone just as clearly from these writings, as far as the early Christians were concerned, as from the epistle of Jude or the Apocalypse. Clearly the inner witness of the Holy Spirit is not alone a sufficient guide for ascertaining the objective value of the apostolic Scriptures in the face of all the influences of purely subjective feeling. The decisive factor was, as has already been said, the preservation of evidence of the apostolic origin and character of the Scriptures – a preservation effected through the people of the Church with the support of the Spirit. And this same authority of the Church in the Holy Spirit, which guaranteed the compiling of the Canon, is seen in the valid and binding declarations of doctrine which the Councils formulated against the Arians. There is no difference in the infallible guidance given in each case. If it is accepted that the compilation of the Canon is the work of the Holy Spirit in the Church it necessarily follows that the doctrinal declarations of the General Councils are the work of the Spirit too. And if the decisions of the General Councils from the fourth to the seventh century are considered to be binding and

---

[43] A. Harnack, *The Origin of the New Testament* (1925), p. 114.

86

inspired by the Spirit of Christ, it is surely impossible not to see this as a constant intervention of the Spirit, according to Christ's promise, throughout all ages. It is the Catholic belief that the solemn doctrinal decisions of the Church take place by virtue of the same presence of the Spirit as the first Council of apostles in Jerusalem. This is the belief of the Fathers of the Church[44] and of the early Councils.[45] At the first Council the work of the Spirit was that of founding the deposit of faith, in post-apostolic times of preserving it. It is the Catholic view that the chronology of this world is always affected by the presence of the risen Lord and is always under the influence of the Spirit, who is tied neither to space nor to time, but who impinges upon our time from his glorified dimension or from the "eternal now", so that the Fathers called him the very "soul of the Church".[46]

In fact to take "Scripture" alone as the criterion and disregard the apostolic succession and its power of preserving the unity of faith is unintentionally to adopt a different attitude to faith from that which characterized the apostolic era. The apostles came to believe through actually living and being with Christ; the early communities believed through "hearing" which presupposes "preachers" who "are sent" (Rom. 10:14). It is true that the apostolic word is to be enshrined in Scripture and so

[44] Clement of Rome, *Ad Cor.* 56, 1; Irenaeus, *Adv. haer.* 3, 24, 1; Cyprian, *Ep.* 24, 5; Augustine, *Serm.* 354.
[45] Council of Ephesus 431 (Denzinger, *op. cit.,* No. 125); Cyril of Alexandria, *Ep.* 55.
[46] Cf. S. Tromp, *De Spiritu S. Anima Corporis Christi* I–II (1932).

become, as Pius XII said, the ultimate foundation for the later preaching of the word, but the actual preaching will always be necessary, in our Lord's words, "for those who are to find faith in me through their word" (John 17:20). If the readiness to have faith in men for Christ's sake were in time replaced by obedience to Scripture alone, the structure of faith would have been altered. As Newman says, we can interpret what we read according to our own feelings or according to the opinion of biblical scholars of the time and it is a human temptation to please ourselves in following the written word.[47] Early Christian obedience was directed not towards something written nor towards the community as a whole but towards the leading people in the community – for Christ's sake: "He who listens to you, listens to me" (Luke 10:16). Naturally obedience to the Church extends only far as the Church is speaking in the name of Christ and where in actual individual cases it is obvious that the bearers of office are not doing so (for instance, in the case of Joan of Arc), the love which is due would consist not in obedience to men but in obedience to God.[48]

A further point for consideration is that Jesus gave the growing Church into the care of the apostles against the time when he himself would no longer be visibly present on earth. This mission for the future was in the same sense as the parable in which "a man went on his travels; he called his trusted servants to him and committed his

[47] Newman, *Sermons to Mixed Congregations* (1921), p. 199f.
[48] Acts 4:19; 5:29; cf. Aquinas, *De veritate* q. 17, 3–5.

money to their charge. He gave five talents to one, two to another, and one to another, according to their several abilities, and with that he set out on his journey" (Matt. 25:14ff.). The parable is clear evidence for the Lord's thought that from the time of his leaving this world his authorized representatives should take his place and have authority (of varying extent) in his name. The mission is given for the time during which he will be absent; it is thus an eschatological one. This is how the apostles understood it and for this reason they too appointed men for the time of their departure who should be their representatives according to Christ's mission and promise "until the consummation of the world". Thus there would always remain bearers of the apostolic authority, thus others would come and take over from them – not as apostles but as leaders of the Church who would preserve Revelation in the communion of faith. The early apostles laboured and it is their labours that those who come later inherit (John 4:38).

We now come to the question of the Petrine office in the circle of apostles, the question whether the authority given by the Lord to Peter was only a personal one and so no official succession should be assumed. This is, in general, how Protestant theologians explain the special powers given to Peter. It is true that Christ speaks directly to Peter and only indirectly to his successors. Peter was singled out from the others because of his confession of faith. But this only tells us something of the occasion which Christ used in order to safeguard something important and fundamental for his Church. His first concern may have been for the foundation of the Church, but after that it was for the Church's structure and its permanent and basic function. He concerned himself with the things of God in the future because he knew he would soon be taken away from the world and his disciples. These concerns are closely connected with, and immediately follow, the promise of the primacy in Matthew 16. His only concern was the Church, the rule of God over the people of God and, through this, the coming of the kingdom of God in the world. His aim and purpose were clearly to make provision for the Church not just for the time immediately ahead, but for all time. He saw in his mind the devil at work; the enmity of the powers of this world was but the foreground he used to indicate to the disciples the vision of the end of time (Matt. 24). The evil spirits of the underworld will ever be on the attack and Christ will ever make provision for his Church, for the end of time, so long as the onslaught lasts. The living rock of strength will be there for ever, not only the memory of the dead Christ.

Or should we assume that Jesus intended the Church, as a small body, to need an instrument of unity, such as the rock, against the onslaught of the underworld; but to need it no longer when later she becomes the Church of the nations? But the Church of apostolic times was more than a community of brothers in the Spirit of love. She was characterized at the same time by a sacred order, a hierarchy in the original sense of the word, by a collegium which directs and guides in the same Holy Spirit. And among this group, all of whom have authority, one is the first, who has "the keys of the kingdom", who governs as chief shepherd for the "lambs and sheep". All this is designed by the Church's Lord for the sake of God's rule, that the Church as the united people of God be the instrument for the coming of his kingdom. How then could the apostles have thought that the Church would later no longer need the same order, the same structure; that she could change according to what seemed best in human terms, according to "human law", to another structure; that later on she would no longer need to be both charismatic and hierarchic; that even in another form she would still be the same Church in keeping with the mind of Christ, because Christ was concerned with the spirit and not with the structure? But if this were so, why did Christ himself lay down a form?

The Church of the first centuries, the apostolic and post-apostolic Church in both East and West, believed itself bound to a certain form. From time to time through the laying-on of hands by the apostolic shepherds, with the co-operation to a certain extent of the community, new members were added among those who wielded authority. If this sacred order were disturbed, as for instance in Corinth at the end of the first century, it was restored by an authority, which was based on the "foresight" of the apostles.[49] This authority takes "precedence in love and represents the law of Christ and the name of the Father"[50] and before this authority "the faithful from

---

[49] Clement of Rome, *Ad Cor.*, 44 ff.
[50] Ignatius of Antioch, *Ad Rom.*, intro.

all around" assemble, in order to give their assent to it as the authoritative rule of the Church's teaching tradition.[51] All this stemmed from the early Church's belief that the "sacred order" provided by the Lord for the beginning of the Church, should remain for future generations too.

The dialogue betwen Jesus and Peter reported in Luke 22:31f. is of great importance for the Petrine primacy. According to this passage, on the last evening just before he hints at Peter's coming denial of him, Jesus says: "Simon, Simon, behold Satan has claimed power over you all, so that he can sift you like wheat: but I have prayed for thee that thy faith may not fail; when, after a while, thou hast come back to me, it is for thee to be the support of thy brethren." E. Stauffer rightly regards this evidence in Luke as revealing Peter's special position among the apostles.[52] Jesus entrusts Peter with a mediatory office among his brethren. The basis and strength of this office will be the sacerdotal mediatory prayer of Jesus, and in it also is grounded the disciple's trust. Any claim of human conceit and arrogance is meaningless from the outset, because everything is accomplished through the mediation of the divine High Priest. From this springs certainty. Even if the occasion on which the words were said is unique and conditioned by the situation at the time, they are fundamental for the Church, especially for "the servant of the servants of Christ" who has the primary responsibility. For the whole basis of his authority is the

[51] Irenaeus, *Adv. haer.* III, 3, 2.
[52] *Theologie des N. T.* (1948), p. 16.

merciful power of God and the presence and mediation of the heavenly High Priest.

Even among Protestant theologians there are some who would not question the biblical basis of the sacred office. They are merely questioning whether what confronts us in history as derived from Christ, is really the sacred office according to the mind of Christ. Emphasis on episcopal responsibility is widespread and even the idea of succession, as we stated it above, is widely accepted and not only for reasons of practical expediency. The chief difficulty, however, we are told again and again, is the Petrine office in its historical form. It is not that the religious character of recent popes is questioned. What is at stake is "the Roman system" as it is called, the outer form of the concept as it has developed in history, beginning with the temporal claims of the popes in the papal states and the power of the Church in contrast with the declining faith of the Middle Ages, up to the present-day centralization of canon law, which, for instance, in the election of bishops implies the minimal co-operation of the actual diocese. Equally obnoxious is found the fact that binding definitions on matters of faith have been issued during the last hundred years not just in order to refute heresies but for the encouragement of piety. These matters are considered to deepen the spiritual rift between the Catholic Church and her separated brethren and to overlook the realization of unity, commanded by the Lord (John 17:20ff.).

As far as these objections are concerned, and they are not to be taken lightly, there are some things which seem to have been overlooked, or not sufficiently realized in the spirit of Christ. While calling attention to these, we are not concerned with being in the right or indeed with sitting in judgment upon those who are hesitant, but simply with Christian sincerity, of which we too are in need.

It is true that the sacred office as we see it in history is far from coinciding with the idea: as one might expect. There is no doubt that on the eve of the Reformation – which indeed lasted throughout the late Middle Ages – the hierarchy was morally and religiously far removed from the spirit which Jesus had demanded from those who held his authority. And later on, too, we must admit that as far as the Church's development was concerned "many distortions, shifts in balance and changes of stress found their way not only into the teaching of individual theologians but also and especially into the Church's practice and were the cause of grave aberrations in her development".[53] Even in the early Middle Ages, during the first stages of the tragic separation of the Eastern and Western Churches, the real roots of the schism lay in "the quarrels of the disciples about rank, about who was the greater" and this was what finally caused it. In the Western world during the late Middle Ages, the struggles and rivalries between popes and antipopes and the secularization brought by the Renaissance among other things resulted in the hierarchy concerning itself more with worldly culture, church government, and

[53] F. X. Arnold, *Theologie der Seelsorge* (1949), p. 63.

94

fiscal matters than with the business of sanctification and renewal. J. Lortz and H. Jedin, well-known historians of the Reformation era, have shown that the losses and defects of the Church at the time were not only due to moral faults but touched the very structure of the Church. The papacy no longer had the moral authority to settle peaceably the conflict about reform and belief which was beginning to break out; only a General Council could have dealt with it and this was not wanted. According to these two historians, events might have been very different had the atmosphere been right for a General Council in 1520–25. The quarrel would then have remained within the Church. In fact it was left to rulers and local governing bodies to decide whether or not their territories should go over to the reformers, whether or not there should be congregations with Mass and bishop. That was the real division of the Church brought about by political powers. In the following centuries the two wings of Western Christianity, in many places divided into Protestant and Catholic areas, became estranged from one another. The awareness of a common and fundamental unity which as yet existed in faith and sacraments was largely concealed and forgotten in mutual polemics.[54] As Professor Jedin put it: "For this reason it is not just differences of doctrine which divide Catholic and Protestant but a long history and a wall of traditions – including hostile instruction and education – which are not perhaps of a theological kind, but which are of great

---

[54] An interesting survey is given by Van der Pol, *Phänomenologie des Protestantismus* (1955), chap. II.

importance in real life. It would be sheer intellectualism to see the problem of a divided Christendom simply from the viewpoint of belief and theology: they are, as it were, the underground factors, not those generally encountered on the surface."

Catholics must, therefore, endeavour to understand the widespread resentment against the hierarchy from the psychological viewpoint too. Moreover, they must not fail to appreciate that behind polemical passion there is often true Christian feeling: there must be no "masters", only one is your master. There must be no self-aggrandizement among those who truly follow the Lord. Responsibilities are received from the Lord, so that men should forget themselves and serve the kingdom of God. Authority and dignity, as images of Christ, should speak for themselves.

What conclusions follow from this for Christians? The answer of the Catholic teaching is that the blemishes in the realization of the sacred office must not leave us indifferent, but bind us in faith to bear witness to the truth of Christ. The truth is that all members of the Church are brothers, even if all do not have the same responsibilities, and no one by invoking Christ may set himself up to "domineer over your faith" (2 Cor. 1:24), for all are hearers of the Word of God and all are bound by it. And if an individual should feel the temptation to boast of himself or regard himself as alone being truly devout, all the "presbyters in your company" (1 Pet. 5:1) and all Christians are not only justified but even bound in duty for Christ's sake as witnesses of the kingdom of God and as spiritual men (1 Cor. 2:15) to remind such a one that he too is a man of flesh and blood. The Lord prayed for Peter precisely because he was the first among the brethren, and so stood in particularly strong temptation, that his faith, his devotion to the Lord and the brethren, might not fail. To pray is to make intercession for something which is not given automatically because it is dependent upon personal humility, faith and love. And "the stewards of God's mysteries" know that "they will have an account to give" (1 Cor. 4:1f.; Heb. 13:17).

In considering the concept of the priesthood it is essential to guard against reverting to a false idealism, which unconsciously starts out from the pre-supposition that, if not in all her members then at least in her official representatives, the Church should be composed of angels! In warning the apostles not to be like the lords of this world, but to make themselves "servants" among his followers, Jesus was surely not guilty of an utopian view of reality (Matt. 20:25). On the contrary, he reckoned with reality. Peter himself was not without weaknesses and for this reason the Lord prayed for him especially. And just as the Lord made allowance for human weakness amongst his close disciples, so he does for the rest of the faithful – including us. Who among us may cast the first stone? Who will demand from anyone the holiness of Christ himself as a condition of the validity and legality of his office? The parable of the net with good and bad fish, of the chaff amidst the corn, of the unfaithful servant who is hard on his fellow-servants and who is punished on his master's return, these are all sufficiently clear. As Newman says: "Scripture more commonly speaks of the Divine design and

97

substantial work, than of the measure of fulfilment which it receives at this time or that."[55] He was referring to St. Paul's telling the Ephesians that they were "chosen out, in Christ, before the foundation of the world, to be saints, to be blameless in his sight, for love of him" (Eph. 1:4).

There are sayings and maxims in abundance which point to the mixture of the divine with the human, the all-too-human. "A great house, besides its plate of gold and silver, contains other objects made of wood and earthenware" (2 Tim. 2:20). Confusions are prophesied so great "that, if it were possible, even the elect would be deceived" (Matt. 24:24). Belief and unbelief, humility and pride, love and selfishness have, from the times of the apostles up to the present day, been present in one body and no human means can separate them one from the other. "And naturally these scandals are the greater, the greater and wider the sphere in which they manifest themselves and they are the more shocking, the more the claim of sanctity and honour places the shepherds of the flock above the rest." That even the apostolic Church was not without outward blemish in this respect is shown by the excesses of mysticism and the moral scandals in Corinth, the Galatians' confusion of doctrine, the solemn admonition of St. Paul on his departure from Miletus (Acts 20:29), the warnings of the pastoral letters, the terrifying picture in the third epistle of St. John of the conduct of a presbyter, the grave tone of the letters to the Christian communities

[55] Newman, *Parochial and Plain Sermons* II, 8.

in the Apocalypse. Whenever the Christians are admonished to bear witness to the truth, they are at the same time admonished to practise prudence or sobriety and this is a theme which recurs frequently in the epistles: "Rid your minds, then, of every encumbrance, keep full mastery of your senses, and set your hopes on the gracious gift that is offered you when Jesus Christ appears . . . Yes, all mortal things are like grass, . . . but the word of the Lord lasts for ever" (1 Pet. 1:13, 24).

A great deal of historical one-sidedness in the development of the Church cannot be ignored. Yet though our attitude to the concept of the sacred office must find its yardstick in the apostles' preaching of the word, it would, nonetheless, be completely contrary to the sense of Holy Scripture if we thought we could carry over into the present age the form of the early Church at any one particular time – and indeed, the Church herself regards any such attempt as a delusion.[56] For, in contrast to mystical systems, the Christian religion rests upon historical foundations. Through the incarnation the saving act of God entered the time-space world. The kingdom of God is "like a grain of mustard seed, that a man has taken and sowed in his ground . . . and it grows into a tree" (Matt. 13:31 ff.). Even in the development of the early Church, which grew up in close historical contact with the people of the Old Testament, we find that someone from among the "presbyters" would be raised to be "bishop". This development was indubitably envisaged by Christ who "in designing the work, designed also its

[56] Denzinger, *op. cit.,* No. 1501–08.

legitimate results".[57] The same is true of the different stages of development of the Petrine office and it would be fundamentally unsound – since it would contradict the essential nature of the Church as the body of Christ in history – to judge the function of the original primacy according to the present-day standards and vice versa.[58] Although Revelation indeed ended with the apostles, it remains an historically efficacious and continuing force. The outward forms vary while the principles remain of the same type and have the same continuity and although both apostles and lay witnesses together represent the Church, it inevitably happens that in the course of the Church's historical development the stress is at times more on the charismatic-prophetic element and at other times more on the institutional character. In his *Summula* Father Przywara wrote in 1953: "What constitutes the vital element of the Church is her ability to move between two poles of tension while rejecting at the same time both episcopalianism and papalism. If the early Christian extreme came close to an obliteration of the primacy, the modern extreme approaches a cancellation of episcopal authority. Yet neither the one nor the other indicates a permanent rule." What matters, in other words, is that time-bound phenomena again and again must find their yardstick in the revelation of Christ.

Finally, everybody may reflect with benefit on the following: "(Thus) the heart of every Christian ought to re-

[57] Newman, *Development of Christian Doctrine* I, 2, 2.
[58] B. Bartmann, *Lehrbuch der Dogmatik* II ([8]1952), p. 169.

present in miniature the Catholic Church, since one Spirit makes both the whole Church and every member of it to be His Temple. As He makes the Church one, . . . so He makes the soul one, in spite of its various affections and faculties, and its contradictory aims. As He gives peace to the multitude of nations, who are naturally in discord one with another, so does He give an orderly government to the soul, and set reason and conscience as sovereigns over the inferior parts of our nature. . . . Till we look at home, no good shall we be able to perform for the Church at large; . . . 'Physician, heal thyself.' . . . Let us but raise the level of religion in our hearts, and it will rise in the world. He who attempts to set up God's kingdom in his heart, furthers it in the world."[59]

[59] Newman, *Subjects of the Day* (1909), pp. 132–4.

The Priesthood:
Mission and Meaning*

To TALK of the priesthood and of the joyful longing for it from his earliest youth, must surely be one of the most gladdening experiences for any servant of the Divine. And yet, in doing so, he would be ill at ease. Nor could he make light of his love. Words would fail him for their inadequacy to express his feelings, as they would anyone under the very eyes and in the very presence of the Eternal High Priest. He would prefer to remain silent, rather than to speak of his relationship with him, for it is not only his words that halt him, his love and reverence are themselves small by comparison with the exaltedness of the object of their devotion. Thus, he can but keep modestly and humbly to the Word of God.

Not being a school-book, but the living Word of God, Holy Scripture does not, generally speaking, give us any facile answer even to the most important religious truths.

* The first part of this paper up to page 112 is from an address given by Dr. Leo Kunz at an ecumenical congress.

An exception would seem to have been made for the priesthood. There is a sentence in St. Paul's epistle to the Hebrews which we may well take to be an actual definition: "The purpose for which any high priest is (1) chosen from among his fellow-men, and (2) made a representative of men in their dealings with God, is (3) to offer gifts and sacrifices in expiation of their sins" (Heb. 5:1).

The first part of the quotation is the easiest to understand. Every priest is "chosen from among his fellow-men". Indeed he must be human and know from his own experience of the weakness and folly of men, so that he really can speak for them (Heb. 5:2). Even those who normally hold themselves aloof from anything religious would expect a priest to show a really human and kindly understanding.

The second part of the quotation could seem less obvious to men of our times, be they of a sympathetic disposition only or of deeper religious feelings. We are accustomed to think of the priest as God's ambassador to men, someone who has to teach, console, and exhort them. But Holy Scripture regards him as someone set apart among men, who presents their petitions to God. The restless spirit of our era does not know what to make of this. It is only on its homeward journey to God that the soul begins to realize the meaning of a prayer said on its behalf. Then, with Gertrud von le Fort, it might say: "You alone truly sought my soul! Who could decry the rightness of your faithfulness? The clever people of this world betrayed it. When it thirsted, they gave it forgetfulness and when it was troubled they said: No, not you!

They advised recourse to reason, as if my soul were an idea. ... But you prayed for my soul and that saved it. You offered sacrifice for it and on this it throve." It is true that the priest is sent to men as their teacher and doctor too, but that is only the result of his central mission. He is a priest above all when he is praying for his fellow-men.

It is, however, the third part, the definition of the priesthood which we find most difficult. Even if we accept intercessory prayer as the priest's chief duty, we still see him foremost in our mind's eye as the priest who, in the midst of his community, joins in with them and for them in antiphonal prayer. But this epistle presents us with an entirely different picture for our prototype of the priesthood: the High Priest of the Old Covenant, who distances himself from the people with the sacrificial gift and enters beyond the heavy curtain of the Holy of Holies into the darkness before the face of the Most High, while the crowd of people wait outside and silence envelops the scene. This may seem strange to us. But the epistle to the Hebrews stresses this side in the life of Christ so much, even at the expense of his actual influence and teachings, that it was at one time thought necessary to distinguish between the Christ seen in this epistle and the historical figure of Jesus. In fact the gospels bear equally cogent witness to our Lord's gradual breaking-away, first from the people, to whom he speaks only in parables; then from the disciples, who find his sayings hard; and in the end from the apostles, to whom he had still much to say which was beyond their reach as yet (John 16:12); and last of all from the three best loved disciples, whom he leaves a little way behind him, while alone he prostrates himself calling out from the depths of his heart: "My Father, if it is possible, let this chalice pass me by; only as thy will is, not as mine is." Our redemption was not wrought by a single word nor by a single act, but by the complete surrender of his body to be broken, of his spirit to be spilt, of his soul with the words: "Father, into thy hands I commend my spirit"; in short, by the consummation of the sacrifice.

In order to understand the significance of sacrifice in the priesthood, we must go back to the beginning of the history of mankind and approach the fulfilment in Christ as it were from afar.

The priesthood and the sacrifice are concepts that pre-suppose a gulf between creator and creation. After the link between man not as yet fallen and his creator was severed by original sin, the children of the banished parents of the human race tried to draw closer to the Almighty once again by way of a gift and outward sign of their good will. They bore it to the altar before the face of God and waited hopefully to see if the face of the wrathful Lord would become calm and if he would accept the symbol of their good will, sanctify it by his acceptance and share it with them at a brotherly meal showing that the inner communion between them had been restored. But even in the case of this first sacrifice we experience in full uncertainty as to whether or not God does in fact accept this gift. Man senses that the outward gift which he brings with him cannot appease God. He wants to demonstrate his devotion and so invol-untarily admits that he is incapable of giving the real gift

105

that God requires, namely his whole heart. For it is easy to scatter a part of one's heart on the things of this world but hopelessly hard to gather it together again and offer it wholly to God. And this uncertainty was so tormenting that one of Eve's sons slew his brother because he could not bear the thought that his brother's sacrifice, that is his heart, should be more pleasing to God than his own.

The fact that subsequently the sacrificial act was the prerogative first of the heads of families, then of the leaders of a people, and finally of a priestly caste is at least partly a concomitant phenomenon of different social systems: the community as well as the individual wished to offer the sacrifice through their representative. The exclusion of the private sacrifice was also partly due to the disturbing question: "Who is worthy to draw near to God?" (cf. Jer. 30:21) – the Hebrew word "kohen" means "the one who draws near to God" – and the answer became clearer and clearer: No man can take the authority upon himself, but only the man who, like Aaron, had received a call from above, from God himself. Only very few, the elect, were called and of these perhaps only one man once a year dared to penetrate into the Holy of Holies, while the hierarchy of priests and the people could only go as far as a certain limit. This distinction served as a reminder of the gulf between God and men.

But at the same time as this hierarchy of mediators was to bridge the gulf between the Creator and his creatures, the realization was dawning that the ladder did not in fact reach the heavens since its rungs were and would remain humans; nor could the consecration, liturgical dress and language disguise what was human, all-too-human in them, for this fact became even more glaringly evident the further they went towards the blinding light of God's presence. The prophets' complaints about priests cannot be ignored. They describe the servants of the sanctuary as fuddled with wine (Is. 28:7), teaching for hire (Mich. 3:11), despising the law (Ez. 23:26), murderers of the prophets (1 Kings 19:10), and a burden to God (Jer. 23:33). Perhaps the reason for such strong reproaches was that they were more conscious of the faults of the priests than of those of other men. Perhaps, too, the rôle of the priests of the Old Covenant was in general a particularly inglorious one, beginning with Aaron who gave in to the pleas of the people and moulded the golden calf, up to Caiphas who bestowed official sanction on the envy of the Pharisees and Scribes and so pronounced the sentence of death on the Son of God. For it seems that there is no stronger temptation to arrogance and lust for power, to irreverence and unscrupulousness, than that which is presented by a religious hegemony.

Throughout the history of Revelation the longing grew for the one High Priest who would be "holy and guiltless and undefiled, not reckoned among us sinners, lifted high above all the heavens" (Heb. 7:26) and yet be wholly man "fashioned as we are, only sinless" (Heb. 4:15). The epistle to the Hebrews sees this longing for the *pastor angelicus* fulfilled in Christ, the High Priest, exalted above all the angels. He was not consecrated by any outward anointing, but by the union of the divine and human natures in the

107

person of the Eternal Word. He bridges the gap between God and man not as one who raises himself up above his brothers, but as one who lowers himself and, in spite of being the Son of God, becomes obedient unto death. He does not glorify himself but renounces the glory before him and chooses the most dishonourable shame of the cross. He does not bear the sign of his good will in an external offering but consummates his all-embracing, loving surrender on the cross in the name of mankind, so to enter into the Holy of Holies, with the sacrificial gift of his wounded body, not through the man-made curtains of the temple (all this was shadow and symbol only), but through the wall dividing time and eternity, God and man, in order to offer the sacrifice for our intercession to his Father, in the person of the Eternal High Priest.

The writer of the epistle to the Hebrews cannot rejoice enough in this fulfilment and he emphasizes again and again that thereby every other high-priestly function has been made superfluous; for the value of this sacrifice is complete and nothing can increase or surpass it, since it is made eternal in the heavenly priesthood of Jesus Christ.

Seen in this light it seems almost a betrayal of Christianity to begin speaking once again of any human priesthood. Are we not thereby reopening the gulf which Christ closed once and for all in order again to bridge it with an earthly hierarchy, which though a link, yet fails to unite men in their contact with God? Do we not conjure up again the diabolical temptation of a lordly clerical caste, when God has offered himself as our only Lord and mediator? Is it not better for us all to stand at a distance and give to him alone the honour? Yes – and yet, no.

He alone is the High Priest – but this does not mean that we must keep our distance. We are called upon to enter not merely in spirit, but through the altar, for what we have is an altar (Heb. 13:10) which represents for us under temporal forms the eternal sacrifice of the heavenly High Priest, for our "approach now is Mount Sion, is the heavenly Jerusalem, city of the living God; here are gathered thousands upon thousands of angels, here is the assembly of those first-born sons whose names are written in heaven, here is God sitting in judgment on all men, here are the spirits of just men now made perfect; here is Jesus, the spokesman of the New Covenant, and the sprinkling of his blood, which has better things to say than Abel's had" (Heb. 12:22–4). We are called to enter into the priesthood of Jesus Christ, into his death and into his resurrection. This is why the Church ordains that the relics of a martyr should be set into every altar (for the altar is a symbol of Christ, the Proto-martyr). Perhaps we would not describe as "priesthood" this entering into the sacrifice of Christ, if Holy Scripture did not use the same term to describe the blessed in heaven and the saints on earth (Apoc. 5:10; 1 Pet. 2:9), just as it used it to describe the chosen people of the Old Covenant (Ex. 19:6). And in the epistle to the Hebrews this parallel is deliberately emphasized when it says: At that time the people did not dare to approach the mountain and "Moses said, in terror at the sight, I am overcome with fear and trembling". At that time the voice of God made the earth rock, but now his promise is that "it shall happen again only once; he will shake earth and heaven too ... Let us worship God as he would have us worship him, in awe and reverence; no doubt of it, our God is a consuming fire" (Heb. 12:18–29). The essence of the priesthood of all believers is the personal participation of the individual Christian in the complete sacrifice of Jesus Christ, the one High Priest, who unites us all with one another and with the Father in a communion of eternal life.

Christ has, in addition, appointed men for the visible worship of God as the stewards and ministers of his mysteries (1 Cor. 4:1), but perhaps we should not call them priests, for Holy Scripture does not. They are indeed but instruments who carry out the outward signs of Christ's mission and by virtue of which alone the High Priest's function becomes effective. Yet, we must remember that the Christian peoples looked upon those who distributed to them the body of the Lord and who undertook for them the sacrificial act as *sacerdotes* in a special sense – as those who offer what is holy – without abandoning the belief in the one priesthood of Jesus Christ. And we can say that it would never have occurred to anyone to dispute their office or title, if all had always remained conscious of being but instruments, servants, of whom nothing is expected except that they should be found trustworthy (1 Cor. 4:2). Moreover, Christ's priesthood is essentially a descent and a service and anyone who feels called to participate more deeply in his priesthood must all the more be penetrated by his spirit. For it was no meaningless gesture when, the night before he gave to his

110

apostles the command, "Do this in commemoration of me", the Lord laid aside his outer garments, girded himself with a towel, and like the humblest servant washed their feet. And when they tried to stop him, he said: "Do you understand what it is I have done to you? You hail me as the Master and the Lord; and you are right, it is what I am. Why then, if I have washed your feet, I who am the Master and the Lord, you in your turn ought to wash each other's feet" (John 13:12ff.); and elsewhere he says: "So it is that the Son of Man did not come to have service done him; he came to serve others, and to give his life, as a ransom for the lives of many" (Matt. 20:28).

If this spirit of Christ had filled the majority of the priests at the time of the Reformation, it would never have occurred to anyone to do away with the special priesthood in favour of the priesthood of all believers. But many of them forgot the saying of Christ that they were not lords and began to feel secure in their rôle and to abuse the sacred office to satisfy their human needs: avarice, ambition, lust for power. And so they succumbed to that greatest of all temptations, with which the devil dared to approach even the Messiah, as Jesus recounted as a warning and example to his disciples. Yet although we must recognize the greatness of the danger, we must not seek to evade the vocation to participation in the priesthood of Jesus Christ. The only thing we can do is to implore the Eternal High Priest to foster in us the great gratitude and reverence which are due, indeed, to his holy mysteries. Above all, to ask that he will fill "the servants and stewards of God's mysteries" with the spirit of his service, so that they will be of a kind and understanding mind in their human way and at the same time be so wholly given up to the Lord that human weakness can no longer hurt them. We must pray that the spirit of Christ will fill them and free them inwardly so that, of their own free will and under no duress they will echo the words of St. Paul: "Not that we would domineer over your faith; rather, we would help you to achieve happiness" (2 Cor. 1:23). Then the image will be realized which St. Ignatius, bishop and martyr, used in his letter to the Ephesians: "Your priests are united to the bishop as the strings are to a zither. But you yourselves are the choir which takes up the melody of Christ and through him sings to the Father with one voice, so that he knows you are the members of his son" (*Ep. ad Eph.* 4).

*

It is far from easy to talk about the priest's mission. It is true that in the Catholic Church the people feel a special reverence for the sacred office – a reverence which is as much in the tradition of the Eastern Church as in that of the West and is an integral part of the "mind of the Church". Many have a deep and sincere devotion to the sacraments and gratitude for what they have received for themselves and their children in the sacramental sphere through the personal service of good pastors; and many mothers can think of no greater happiness in life than to see one of their sons standing at the altar as a priest. In contrast to these, however, there are, even among Catholics, many who speak of the "reverend gentlemen" coldly and with many reservations, critically and even bitterly – as a result of disappointments – or who, sometimes quite legitimately, make a sharp distinction between the sacred office and its human occupants. As far as the majority of our Protestant fellow-Christians are concerned, they feel, in spite of their admiration for individual priests, a definite antipathy towards the office and this feeling has a religious basis, for in Protestant teaching it is the "priesthood of all believers" which is stressed and the spiritual office is seen as a purely human form, as a natural necessity of community life, or even as a human usurpation which strikes at Christian freedom and the charismatic brotherhood of all men.

The Catholic priest will not feel this to be a personal affront. In fact, it makes him proof to a far greater degree than ever before against the possible temptation of choosing a vocation for the sake of human respect, which is considered as foolishness in the purely human sense. I think that few men become priests today except for Christ's sake alone – those who have any other reason are quite simply to be pitied.

To understand the meaning and importance of the priesthood in the spirit of the Catholic Church, it is essential to start from Christ – what he was and what he intended to be. For it is part of the Catholic faith that the priesthood goes back to him; its power is derived from his mission and his authority. Jesus explained that his mission was to proclaim the reign of God, the rule of God in man and in God's people and to procure for us the graces of this reign. God was to be recognized by men as the Lord and Father of love and "adored in spirit and in truth"; and Christ came because we men were lost in the blindness of self-love and could not find our way unaided and alone; he, the beloved Son in whom God was well pleased, the High Priest of God, came to lead home erring and bewildered humanity, "to search out and to save what was lost" (Luke 19:10). To do this Jesus did not simply come himself, he also chose messengers for the glad tidings and gave them authority and promised them his support until the end of time: "You, therefore, must go out, making disciples of all nations, and baptizing them ... teaching them to observe all the commandments which I have given you. And behold I am with you all through the days that are coming, until the consummation of the world" (Matt. 28:19f.).

Nowhere in the New Testament does Jesus lay his hands solemnly and deliberately on the apostles and consecrate them, at the same time enumerating their priestly powers and duties and explaining how they should hand on the consecration. Rather he lets the demands of God's kingdom slowly penetrate and develop in their consciousness, and the new proceed out of the old. In the same way he never puts himself forward and proclaims himself amid scenes of pomp as the Messiah and King, as was imagined by the messianic tradition, but gradually unfolds the secret of his mission to his trusted disciples in intimations and indirect corrections of their human notions. So also the Church of Christ developed, like a gradual budding from scattered seeds, with the slow and almost secret preparation of the disciples, the future foundation stones of the new house of God, for their public life which began on the day of Pentecost. The priesthood of the New Testament follows this pattern. Holy Scripture only dares to use the name "priest", so maligned in religious history, and then hesitantly, in a phrase in the epistle to the Hebrews and the first epistle of St. Peter and then only of Christ himself, the one anointed priest, and of his holy people in general, because only in this context is any suggestion of the glorification of self or the seductive aura of human dignity and human glory completely avoided. But those things which ancient tradition had piously expected of the order of Melchisedech, namely the consecration of human life under the symbol of bread and wine by that mysterious priest-figure, whose lineage was of no account (Heb. 7), were fulfilled in the perfect consecration of the human race through him who offers himself in ransom to the Father as their head and acts as their mediator. In order that they might "do this in commemoration" of him, Christ formed spiritually those disciples given to him by the Father then as now and commanded them to preach the salvation of all through him and to go forth as a sacerdotal nucleus among the people of God.

When the first disciples met him beyond the Jordan and when they were called from their nets on the sea of Galilee, they did not know where they were going: "Come and see!" (John 1:39.) "And they dropped their nets immediately, and followed him" (Matt. 4:20). They were, however, given an unprecedented sign: "Stand out into the deep water and let down your nets for a catch." –

115

"Master, we have toiled all night and caught nothing; but at thy word I will let down the net." And God performs the impossible, in the face of which man can only say: "Leave me to myself, Lord; I am a sinner" (Luke 5:4–9).

This is what inevitably happens when God's call comes to man. He feels the gulf which separates the creature from his Creator, the sinner from infinite holiness. The Lord has no reason to dismiss Peter's self-accusation of sinfulness, but he does not show any interest in it either. He simply says: "Do not be afraid." Although you are what you are, you have nonetheless been called, "Henceforth thou shalt be a fisher of men" (Luke 5:10). Since it is the Lord's will, to be afraid would be a lack of faith, a sin. For faith glorifies God. He who is called puts his faith in the word of him who calls him and so dares to help his fellow-men and is able to ignore both his own short-comings as a man and the criticisms of others. For the Almighty "can give what he commands, and so can command what he will" (Augustine).

In the course of developments Jesus himself had to recognize – through the mystery of his Father's guidance, and much against his own human wish – that his call to prepare for the kingdom of God had no chance of realization among the people as a whole. Thus came the second stage of the message of the kingdom. Seventy disciples, equal in number to the elders of Israel, were sent by him as messengers to proclaim that the kingdom of God was at hand: "He who listens to you, listens to me; he who despises you, despises me" (Luke 10:16). And when they returned and told of the divine signs which had accompanied their work – they knew beforehand of the hardness of heart of the many since Jesus had prophesied it – Jesus was filled with gladness that the Father had revealed such things "to little children" (Luke 10:21). Next he unfolded the deeper meaning of his doctrine to them in parables, giving them examples of mercy in his deeds and so teaching them firstly the meaning of the power to bind and to loosen (Matt. 18:18) and secondly the meaning of the "cup" which they had to be prepared to drink with him (Matt. 20:22). Then he spoke once more of the Spirit which should animate them: "A disciple is no better than his master, a servant than his lord" (Matt. 10:24) and reminded them that they are not to be like the lords of this world, who vaunt their power over the people (Matt. 20:25). On the last evening he commanded them to celebrate the mystery of the redemption, the symbol of union in his blood as "a commemoration" of him (Luke 22:19); then he breathed on them again: "Receive the Holy Spirit; when you forgive men's sins, they are forgiven ..." (John 20:23); and finally, as he sent them out, he promised them his support "until the consummation of the world" (Matt. 28:20).

The ambassadors of Christ and the "elders", that is presbyters (Acts 14:23), installed by them in the community and consecrated by the laying-on of hands, are "Christ's servants and stewards of God's mysteries" and priests (for so the name *presbyter* was later translated) and what they do for the kingdom of God among their fellowmen, they do in Christ's name and not in their own, on his

117

authority and not on theirs, for his ends not for theirs, by his power and not their own. For there is only one "High Priest" and "mediator", the epistle to the Hebrews tells us. And so we experience the saving and sanctifying powers of his grace through and in Christ alone. He is the sole author, all others are mere instruments. The efficacy of the word or sacrament, therefore, does not depend on the saintliness of any individual human being, but on Christ alone, the one priest and head.

From whatever viewpoint we consider the priest's mission in the service of Christ – either from the human side as spiritual responsibility in a "shell of perishable earthenware" or from the divine side as the imparting of the Spirit and of authority – it is in every case too serious a calling for any man with a vocation to want to make a display of his "dignity" and put on an aura of greatness. Christ the Lord "meek and humble of heart" gave his chosen apostles their sublime mission with the grave admonition: "So it is that the Son of Man did not come to have service done him; he came to serve others and to give his life as a ransom for the lives of many" (Matt. 20:28). Paul often had to emphasize the genuine nature of his mission, but when he comes to talk about the magnitude of his calling, he sees the brilliant countenance of Christ, of the new Moses, and belittles himself, saying only that "we ought to be regarded as Christ's servants, and stewards of God's mysteries". And explaining the meaning he adds: "And this is what we must look for in choosing a steward; we must find one who is trustworthy." For these are unprecedented powers which no man can take unto himself, of which no one can believe a man capable: to share in the power of the keys of him who alone "holds the keys of death and hell" (Apoc. 1:18) and who alone has power to bind and to loose, to reconcile and to sanctify, for he has dedicated himself for the sake of many (John 17:19). How could a human being dare to represent him who represents the Father except in his name which is above all names? But "the man who welcomes one that I send, welcomes me" (John 13:20) and "to see me is to see him who sent me" (John 12:45): thus the only possible attitude for a man is that it is God and not he himself who counts. Otherwise he could not dare to raise his hand in blessing, to speak the words of consecration like the Lord at the Supper, to pass on the words of forgiveness to his fellow-man in Christ's name and to accomplish the humanly impossible in his faith in Christ's power. Thus St. Chrysostom could say: "You must believe that this meal is none other than that in which Christ gave himself to the disciples: it is not men who prepare it but he himself. When you see the priest administering the sacred food, do not think it is a man who does this but know that it is Christ's hand which is stretching out to you."[1] Man performs the rite, God the miracle.

Here, too, we find the reason why the priest wears a supra-personal garment, as it were, during the liturgy; and why he does not speak in a language of his own making nor of his own accord; and why his every movement, his bearing is dictated, not left to his own choice. He speaks and

[1] *In Matt.* 50:3.

acts not personally but as priest for the sanctified, as representative of the risen Christ. It is true that the rites have developed gradually over the years and that there is no need for them to be so rigid, for they were not so initially at the first brotherly gathering, in spite of all the reverence there was for him whom they greeted as their ever-present Lord: "Maran atha – the Lord is coming" (1 Cor. 16:22). The outer ceremonies can be full of pomp in the Byzantine manner, or more austere as in the Roman rite, and could equally well take place with the sobriety favoured by the Northern temperament, but they are removed as far as possible from the secular world to make us conscious that it is not the priest as a man who is acting here but that another is working through him. Over the years a particular kind of life, a position with a special stamp and specific conditions has evolved for the priest – in the Western Church its most striking aspect is celibacy – yet these outer forms are not the same everywhere and are not an essential part of Christ's mission, but are, nonetheless, the obvious expression of the fact that the priest is in a special way called for the service of God's kingdom, that he is called "to leave all", that the servant of the Lord no longer belongs to himself but to the "undivided" service of God.

When the bishop lays his hands upon him at ordination, it is for the priest the same as when the apostles did so to those whom they appointed in agreement with the community. It can happen that inexperienced priests sometimes say far too much and arouse in their amazed or sceptical hearers the painful suspicion that here is a man who possesses powers far greater than the angels – as if a man were anything without the Spirit of him, who desired his servants to say "We are servants and worthless" and to show themselves models of his unselfish love. For a man possesses nothing but what has been lent him, as a responsibility and not for his glory before either God or men. The true priest feels his own unworthiness to be the instrument of the Saviour, himself one who has been saved. But not to have confidence in him who calls would be but an admission of little faith on the part of the man who is called. For the faithful are told that it is the power of Christ's grace in him that they should honour and not the man himself, who is as human as they are. In his own view he is a weak vessel and a poor mouth for divine things. When he speaks the words, which it is his mission to proclaim, to young and old, the educated and the uneducated, it is not on his own wisdom that he draws, he does not refer to his own education or his own human experience. For he knows that many may be superior to him in these respects and that not long ago he was but a boy or youth in their midst and could be asked: "How? Why? With what right?" (as the Nazarenes said of Jesus.) He draws instead on the inexhaustibly profound and sacred "word of life, which proceeds from the mouth of God" and administers graces which are obtained not by magic but as the gifts which the heavenly High Priest wishes him to administer. And when he undertakes to mend a broken reed, to support the troubled conscience, to reassure the sinner of his forgiveness, it is not in reality the man who, himself subject to error and human frailty, presumes to make such a claim, but the envoy in the name of Christ who proclaims peace to the man of divine grace.

There is yet another reason why it would be impossible for the priest who lives in accord with the mind of Christ to exalt himself: to speak of "the dignity of the priest" is only possible at all on the basis of the dignity of all and with a special emphasis on the dignity of those "whom God loves and has called to be holy" (Rom. 1:7), all who are members of the royal and priestly people in Christ. It is here only, in the midst of the initiated body of baptized believers that the priest comes into his own and all are made to share his dignity, unworthy though they may be, in the same way as "a faithless people" is allowed to share the wondrous light which dawned in Christ. Within this grace and dignity of all the holy people, the official priesthood differs only in its function: in so far as all are called upon to have a share in Christ, in the spirit of his abundance, but do not all participate in the same way. Indeed, the difference is essential and permanent: for participation in the general priesthood and the testimony of faith cannot simply develop, by virtue of its own charism, into the authority and dignity of a priesthood administered by solemn ordination. All Christians receive a share in the priesthood of the one heavenly Christ in Baptism and Confirmation: they receive the power and quality of their calling as children of God and members of the communion of saints, "to have life" not only for themselves, but to contribute reciprocally to the spiritual growth of each one according to his own nature and talent. For the Lord promised his Spirit to all his faithful and fulfilled his promise in the coming of the Spirit at Pentecost on the whole community, on "your sons and daughters, my servants and handmaids" (Acts 2:17 ff.), and similarly the messengers from Jerusalem laid their hands on those who had just been baptized in Samaria (Acts 8). Confirmation is the consecration to the general priesthood, of which Peter speaks in his first epistle (5:2ff.) and John in the Apocalypse (5:10). All are called to be "a chosen race, a royal priesthood, a consecrated nation" in private prayer and public worship, in work for the community, in family and career, in bearing witness to the Word and to charity in deed in order "to proclaim the exploits of the God who has called you out of darkness into his marvellous light" (1 Pet. 2:9).

It is undeniable that for too many this practical faith hardly exists in their religious consciousness; it is undeniable that it has for long enough been under-rated in the Catholic world, precisely because it was over-emphasized (at least theologically) on the Protestant side of Christianity. The biblical and liturgical renewal is in the happy process of rediscovering an almost forgotten sense of value in a certain dignity and fellow-feeling for all, which neither fear of false enthusiasm nor undue concern for clerical interests will eventually be able to obscure. In the Church of Christ there is, from the spiritual point of view, strictly speaking, no "laity" in contrast with priests. There are only the priestly people *(laos)* and particular tasks and responsibilities in the official mission within this sphere. In the "communion of saints" all are brothers and sisters with a share in the priesthood. In the mutual prayers for one another, in the communal celebration of the redeeming sacrifice of Christ, in the task of educating the young, in family and school, in brotherly love and kindness, in mutual forgiveness, in the sanctification of conjugal love, in wishing others well, in words and deeds of charity: all these are of equal importance and similarly applicable to all Christian believers in their priesthood, as they are to the particular mission of those who are ordained. What applies to all in their own sphere and measure, applies even more so to the priest in his particular sphere and special responsibility for the community: Christ's promise and his sanctifying grace finds fulfilment in all. All are moulded after the one High Priest and saviour. And we priests who are called by ordination can but beseech you, if you believe in Christ, do not say: they are called, not we – it falls to their lot, not to ours. Rather we must all learn to become fully acquainted with our share in Christ and so bring to fruition what Christ wants to do for the kingdom of God through all those who believe in him.

Here I have in mind, also, the Protestant Christians. For they, too, form part of the body of Christ and are witnesses to the kingdom of God in the world, by the grace of their faith in baptism. They do not share the Catholic conception of the supreme authority of the Church, the power of which was handed down by the laying-on of hands by the apostles and which could never be replaced by assignment on any other promptings of the Spirit. Or rather, it is a concept which is met with uncertainty by some and is completely alien to others. Early Calvinism, before the introduction of its formulae and secularization, was still close to Catholic tradition in refusing to recognize any free call of the Spirit or democratic method of electing pastors and insisted on ordination as an apostolic form.[2] Even Luther did not want simply to do away with the traditional spiritual office of bishops and priests; however, as W. Stählin explains, "since the bishops, as the legitimate holders of the spiritual office, had failed in the work of renewing the Church (in Luther's sense), he saw no other way, since the Church was in a state of distress, than to derive the office from the community, from the priestly mission of every Christian".[3] Seen historically such a reaction is easy to understand as a revulsion against a clergy discredited in their status, but, in view of the clericalism of the late Middle Ages, it was a profound structural change in the opposite direction. It would have required a miracle to strike a happy medium between the two extremes in the acutely inflammatory atmosphere of theological and political strife. Perhaps future ecumenical exchanges between responsible theologians will in time succeed in contributing towards a certain relaxation of tension in those sections of the Christian community where the mistrust in a "system" still exists alongside and in grave conflict with a comparatively small measure of hope and goodwill towards unity in Christ. It seems, too, that the priesthood, in spite of the direct threat from Antichrist, is still not completely proof against the temptation of protecting its own professional interests first and retreating into a cleri-

[2] Calvin, *Instit.* IV, 3–4.
[3] *Vom göttlichen Geheimnis* (1936), p. 101.

calism of which the consequences should by now be obvious.

The heart of the problem lies, as von Campenhausen[4] points out, in the difficulty of ensuring the correct balance between the hierarchical office, the intervention of the Spirit and the responsibility of all believers (Eph. 2:20). For the Church is founded on the principle of interaction and collaboration between apostolic office and the free summons of the Holy Spirit. There were times when one side was unduly emphasized: for long periods of the Church's history the idea of a priestly office was slandered by the extremely unpriestly reality of that office. It is true, however, that even in the clericalism of the Middle Ages the charismatic spirit of prophetic witness did not completely disappear, but there was, nonetheless, lacking that spontaneity which was characteristic of early Christendom and which was its missionary strength. The prophetic witness was often forcibly suppressed by the clergy and there is still a widespread fear among Protestant Christians of a recurrence of a Catholic authoritarian system unworthy of Christians – although the leaders of the Church today make every effort to reawaken an awareness of the importance of the testimony and responsibility of all. It will not be the fear of Antichrist but the spirit of faith and the love of the Lord amongst Christ's sheep that will not only make shepherd and flock feel united and keep them so, but that will also cause the separated Christians to sense their deeper bonds, which not even tragic divisions can com-

---

[4] *Kirchliches Amt und geistliche Vollmacht* (1953), pp. 324f.

pletely obscure. It is indeed the Catholic priest and his Protestant colleague who will have to bear – and bear before God – the main burden of responsibility for the preservation of this deeper consciousness of unity and for its guidance in a spirit of truth and love, in a spirit of mutual trust, through their prayers for one another, through penance for the faults and failings of their forefathers as well as their own and through their faith and hope in the guidance of him who promised to all who believed in him his presence and comfort in suffering.

The Priesthood and Woman

First of all, why is the Church bound by her Eastern and Western tradition not to confer the priesthood upon women? Surely, they are more readily susceptible to religious feeling (which is not suggesting that they are "more religious" altogether), and they represent two-thirds of all church-going Christians. It may always have been so. We find enough references to women in the epistles, and early Christian witnesses speak of the indebtedness to them for their understanding and resourcefulness in furthering the Christian mission and intrinsic life of the Church. We need only to remind ourselves of Paul's acquaintance with Prisca in Corinth, Lydia in Philippi, Phoebe in Rome, and of those "god-fearing" women – the link between the Jewish Christians and the Hellenic mission. The full meaning of St. Paul's reference in the first epistle to Timothy also recalls how much this follower of the Apostles (one of many) owed to his mother from his early youth in matters of religion (even his grand-mother is mentioned). It brings home to us the importance of a mother's care in earliest childhood education with its lasting psychological effect in later life. Moreover, the example of Christ himself is one of exquisite ease, simplicity and unbiassed judgment towards women, so that many followed him with Mary to the cross, with no ulterior motive for a favourable position.

Why not? Certainly not because they were looked down upon by Jesus or by the Apostles and not even by Paul who clearly counsels them "to keep silence" during religious worship, though by no means generally during hours of instruction or devotion. Apart from an occasional reference to Oriental custom, there is never any mention of belittlement. There is "no more male and female" in Christ, no distinction of sex in the primary transcending relationship with God: "you are all one person in Jesus Christ" (Gal. 3:29). Not even Mary, the heart and soul of the Church and of the familiar circle that surrounded the Apostles, who stands for the highest symbol of dignity and compassion, not even she commands a position of authority, although "all generations shall call her blessed" because she was chosen by God. We would even feel it strange, had she wished for it in any way. Why?

Because her feminine sympathy and particular merits in or out of wedlock have already earned her a sufficiently important place in the kingdom of God, a woman might easily be out of her element in any official position of ecclesiastical responsibility. Her natural gifts are, as a rule, more easily directed to a sphere of influence outside any

128

official ecclesiastical administration. She is more at home in her sympathetic approach, as man to man, in her selfless surrender, love, and devotion within the framework of the general priesthood and its sweeping, and infinitely important, domestic influences on the family and Christian society as a whole. Here she is indeed the unobtrusive leader and in her feminine resourcefulness and religious fervour all the more able to follow Mary's example.

Whatever may be her position in the official ministry of the Protestant churches, and here I prefer to make no judgment, I believe that in the Catholic Church the woman has generally come into her own even without the dignity of the priesthood – no doubt partly, but not entirely so, because she is appreciated by the priesthood for her merits, sustained by them in her human and religious outlook more often than not, encouraged in her active interest in the parish and her awareness of an ever widening sphere of influence before her. From a truly zealous priest a woman will receive the sympathetic hearing and the spiritual guidance she requires, particularly in an age that calls for her protection against the tendency of undue masculine demands.

The religious woman will derive much spiritual benefit from the priest's interpretation of the Scriptures and from the sacraments and be assured of a moral support and disinterested counsel that would be hard to find elsewhere. Of course, there is a certain type of misogynist whose overbearing manner often betrays some inward insecurity (the danger in the opposite direction will be dealt with later). But this could hardly apply to the spiritually mature

129

and least of all to a priest. He would be shamed before his own mother and before the Heavenly Mother. Should his natural instinct fail him, the priest's experience would teach him that a woman's intuitive gifts are more profound even if less inclined to solve the most important issues by rational means, but by the assessment of her own experience or the human merits of a situation, relying less on theoretical opinion and more on the practical application of her knowledge. If, on the other hand, the priest has learnt to be more of a psychologist than a mere dogmatist, canonist or moralist – and that is something which his theological studies do not always enable him to be, he will know that it is better not to solve a problem by schematic wisdom without due consideration of the individual circumstances and more intimate questions that affect a woman's private life. He will give her credit for the voice of her own conscience, her intuitive conclusions, sense of honour and responsibility before God, and find that it is more important for a priest to inspire confidence in the mercy of God and help in giving advice, encouragement and comfort, rather than to lay down the law.

There is another point to be considered in discussing "priest and woman". Because a woman, generally, is more sensitive to religious influences, more in need of guidance, approval and support than a man (who is more self-reliant), a priest will find himself giving more of his attention to women. He should not allow himself to be inhibited or embarrassed by cheap gibes about hidden sexual motives. Clearly, there will always be a certain excessive feminine enthusiasm and admiration, especially for the qualities of noble and spiritually distinguished priests – even Mary Magdalen showed this in her own way to our Lord, who was far from rejecting her for it, but full of graciousness for her kind. Indeed how full of meaning were his words for the penitent sinner whose extravagance brought indignation from Simon the Pharisee: "I tell thee, if great sins have been forgiven her, she has also greatly loved" (Luke 7:47). Our Lord himself had deeply touched her heart, his human sympathy having revealed to her also the image of God. Of course, a priest is only human; he cannot claim to have changed his nature in his ordination and he still needs to exercise self-discipline in the awareness of his great responsibility. Some will inevitably come to grief on the point of celibacy, and one would possibly wish for a more lenient canonical consideration of such tragic cases as might leave the Church the poorer for their loss. Others might be in favour of the early Christian view in preference to the law of celibacy, because of the problems this presents in areas such as those of South America and Africa. But no evasion or rejection of celibacy could lead us to ignore the laws of the New Testament. Rather should its recommendations, on the one hand, and its sociological merits, on the other, help us to preserve them. The renunciation of the pleasures of a family in favour of greater freedom of action for the kingdom of God, naturally cuts more deeply across our natural inclinations than any renunciation of material possession. And if we may apply to this the very words of the Apostle

131

who refers to God as having chosen "what the world holds foolish, so as to abash the wise" and "what the world holds weak, so as to abash the strong" (1 Cor. 1:27), we remind ourselves of the example in the personal life of Jesus Christ, his undivided devotion to the kingdom of God and the exacting demands he dared to make of his nearest friends who understood him. John, who was closest to his heart, understood him and so did Paul who recommends this way of life, more like a "true counsellor" than by any "command" from the Lord.

There are two ways open to man, yet both, says the Lord, are beyond man's power fully to realize or achieve. One is the way of perfect wedlock. And here Jesus refers to the original order of things as distinct from the old and the new acceptances of "reason". Not all are able to understand this, nor the other way in which man renounces wedlock for love of the kingdom of heaven (nor is it necessary for everyone to understand the way to which he was not called: "Take this in you whose hearts are large enough for it" [Matt. 19:12]).

In the ancient Jewish religion, we find the Essenes already cherishing celibacy as an ideal condition of excellence and, apart from those early Christians in primitive society who were called upon to practise celibacy, there were others out of wedlock, or widowed, who gave their services to the Church, with charity, in one way or another. Then the ascetic monks spread their influence to both East and West, from Palestine and Egypt, and were highly respected for their religious and moral heroism, being much sought after for their

132

counsel, since they were looked upon as "spiritual fathers". Indeed, their practice was later adopted by the Latin Church (though not necessarily by the Roman Catholic Church alone) as a condition of the priesthood. Its importance for the history of the Church and civilization is considerable. As is well known, the Christians of the East respected the celibate monks more than their married counterparts. Dostojevsky was only one of many who derived much spiritual strength and support from his association with them. The spread of Christianity in our part of the world is undoubtedly greatly due to the work of single-minded Irish and Anglo-Saxon monks and priests, and the whole of our Western culture would be unthinkable without their great contribution, with its far-reaching effect over the centuries. It has the Imitation of Christ at its deepest roots, and we must learn to respect it with a true spirit of love before we can grasp its significance. Not even the knowledge of the danger which is threatening everything sacred or of the inertia which characterizes our age can cast a shadow on what is sublime. For a while the reformers were tempted, because of deplorable lapses, to question the ideal as such, but the ideal – that is, the word of Christ – has withstood the shocks of history, just as the ideal of perfect marriage remains intact, although many fail to attain it. Recognizing this, Protestant Christianity is now undergoing a change, that is likely to admit and to respect celibacy and the monastic life.

Nonetheless, there are always priests who fall from this ideal, although they are in other respects gifted pastors and religious men. God alone can know and judge, and we are

133

all dependent on his mercy – who of us "will cast the first stone"? Canon law, too, is far from setting itself up in the place of the one omnipotent Judge when it enforces strict order. An objective observer will, however, learn of many priests who, perhaps not without crises but with an unquestionable singleness of devotion, combine their religious detachment from human ties with so much understanding and kindness and their inner peace and cheerfulness with so much priestly compassion, that they recall Christ, their model, in their dealings with women.

These priests receive from their contact with women much that is valuable; for there are women who not only themselves gain spiritually from the priest, but also contribute in no small degree to his life and work as man and priest. For woman as guardian and protector of life has an importance and a mission which are all-embracing. The relationship between man and woman in human society is not restricted to the sexual plane in the narrow sense but includes manifold spiritual and intellectual levels of influence and intercourse, of reciprocal fulfilment and enrichment. It is, therefore, only to be expected that the priesthood is not deprived of this, that religious women from Mary onwards, her sisters in the general priesthood, the human channels of Christ's grace, have importance for the priest too. This is not only true of his own mother but of other women too who, inspired by the priestly mission and by a divine providence which they themselves cannot explain, accept the opportunity and the task of helping and strengthening the priest as a man by their womanly and motherly care. They are, as it were, mother

134

and sister in one to him, taking into account both his nature as a man and his loyalty as a priest.

Witnessing these effects in priests, monks and nuns, we realize what prayer and spiritual nearness to the mystery of the altar can achieve. For it is granted them to offer their devotion, the sacrifice of their self-denial, to the Lord for the mystical Body of Christ without therefore despising other men. Anyone who has experienced being, as it were, upheld by unknown forces in his or her spiritual trials, will, like Paul, attribute it to the mystery of the mystical Body, whereby the sacrifices of some of the members benefit the others. Perhaps for this reason St. Augustine and St. Benedict lived in community with their friends and were in close contact with their actual sisters and their sisters' women friends, believing that only good could come of the proximity which recalled that of the men and women who were in the circle of disciples round Jesus.

The priest celebrates Mass for the whole of Christendom and for the people of his own parish, that they may all find, in their different places, light and strength for their pilgrimage. In the Canon of the Mass he prays for the communion of all those who believe in Christ, that the "most gracious Father" will keep and guide his Church in peace and unity throughout the world. Similarly the early Christians prayed at the celebration of the Eucharist: "Perfect, o Lord, thy Church in thy love, and guide her, that has been hallowed, by the help of all the four winds into thy Kingdom, which you are preparing for her. For thine is the glory and the power for ever."

135

The Priesthood of All the Faithful

"THIS HIGH PRIEST of ours is one who has taken his seat in heaven, on the right hand of that throne where God sits in majesty ... there are priests ... who devote their service to the type and the shadow of what has its true being in heaven" (Heb. 8:1, 5).

"You too must be built up on him, stones that live and breathe, into a spiritual fabric; you must be a holy priesthood, to offer up that spiritual sacrifice which God accepts through Jesus Christ .... He has become the chief stone at the corner .... You are a chosen race, a royal priesthood, a consecrated nation, a people God means to have for himself; it is yours to proclaim the exploits of the God who has called you out of darkness into his marvellous light" (1 Pet. 2:5, 9).

"He has proved his love for us, by washing us clean from our sins in his own blood, and made us a royal race of priests, to serve God, his Father; glory and power be his through endless ages, Amen" (Apoc. 1:6).

In the New Testament there is one unique all-embracing

priesthood with only one High Priest of the faithful, who mediates for them. Looking at the various different aspects or offices of this one priesthood of our Lord, it is possible to distinguish them in traditional terminology as the teaching office, the sacerdotal office (specifically the service of the sacraments and the altar) and the pastoral office of Jesus. They are, however, all merely different aspects of the one universal mission of the High Priest, who is both God and man, and of his presence in his Church throughout the ages.

The Church as a whole, the communion of all Christ's faithful as his "bride", is the recipient of his grace and his promise. Individuals receive this grace to the extent that they are incorporated through their faith, of which the sign or seal is holy baptism, and through their life lived according to this faith, in the mystical and real communion of blood and spirit with Christ, the new progenitor of mankind. As a sacrament of consecration with an indelible character baptism is completed by confirmation, the anointing in the Holy Spirit, and is thus the sacrament of ordination for the general priesthood.

All the living members of the mystical Body of Christ share in his threefold office, although to a different degree according to their different gifts and the guidance of the Spirit (1 Cor. 12). They all participate in the one priesthood of Jesus; as the epistle to the Hebrews puts it: "Let us come forward with sincere hearts in the full assurance of the faith" (10:22). This general priesthood of the people is by no means to be understood in a symbolic, as it were poetic sense, as has been suggested by someone recently.

137

It is as far from being simply figurative and poetic, as baptism and confirmation are from being mere symbols without real efficacy.

It is clear from the Acts of the Apostles that the faithful of the early Christian community felt themselves committed and responsible witnesses to the kingdom of God in the world (Acts 4:31). They were consulted by the apostles on all important decisions: for instance, about the choice of Matthias as a replacement (Acts 1:15ff.), about the sending out of Paul and Barnabas on the mission (Acts 13:2ff.), and about the proceedings of the council of apostles (Acts 15). According to Clement of Rome[1] the presbyters were from the very beginning appointed by the apostles or those authorized by them but with the consent of the Church: after the Church's spokesmen had been chosen, the apostles personally installed them in their office through the laying-on of hands (consecration). The same fact emerges from one of the earliest manuals of Church customs, the "Teaching of the Twelve Apostles", according to which the community chose the "bishops and deacons", that is, the spiritual leaders and their assistants, to be consecrated and so in fact decided on the candidates for consecration.[2] This was not only a matter of pastoral prudence, it was the idea of the Church itself which the apostles were following in this respect: a brotherhood with its spiritual offices performed in a spirit of love (John 21:15ff.; 1 Pet. 5:1ff.). Later in the third century Bishop Cyprian wrote to his flock: "I wish

[1] I *Clement* 44.   [2] *Did.* 15.

138

to do nothing without your advice and the consent of the people, nothing on my personal opinion alone", and: "It is seemly that bishops should not only teach but learn too." Then as now there were many men and women amongst the laity well versed in human and religious matters. In the time of the apostles we find Lydia of Philippi, Prisca and Aquila, Phoebe and Thekla, Paul's almost legendary helper, not to mention men like Apollo, Luke, Mark and Silas, as well as the many others surrounding St. Paul, of whom we do not know whether they had received any special degree of ordination (cf. Rom. 16). During the time of the Apostolic Fathers and the Fathers of the Church there were many highly gifted and prominent laymen in the Church's mission: Pantaenus, Origen, Clement of Alexandria, Aristides, Justin, Minucius Felix, Tatian, Tertullian, Arnobius, Lactantius and others. In the early Church the emphasis was far less on the difference, apart from the contrast in state, than on the essential unity of "apostles and prophets", on which the Church is founded (Eph. 2:20).

Only from the time of Constantine onwards, and then to an especially great extent in the Germanic mission, did the position of clerics gain a completely different stamp; this was due to politics. Bishops and abbots were entrusted with state offices and the aristocratic rights of landowners; in return, as nobles privileged from birth, they owed an allegiance to the Emperor which was not always easily reconciled with their pastoral duties. As far as the people and the ordinary priests who served them were concerned, they were lords and superiors and there

139

could be no question in the feudal society of the Middle Ages of the right to discussion and consultation that had existed in the early Church. In addition, education was closely tied to the Latin monastic schools and thus the gulf between teachers and hearers was emphasized. In the time of the early Fathers the most important theologians had for the most part received their classical education while associating freely with mainly pagan teachers and fellow-students at the Hellenic universities of Athens, Caesarea and Alexandria;[3] now the privilege had been passed on to the monastic schools and interest in church affairs was considered to be the prerogative of the clergy – so much so that Cardinal Humbert in the eleventh century, for instance, could term it "presumption" for lay people to take any part in church matters at all. The consequent development of a conflict, even enmity, between clergy and laity was regarded by Boniface VIII in his bulls as a fact to be reckoned with in any realistic policy of the Church.

It would be pointless to evaluate this development only from the viewpoint of its less favourable consequences and merely mark it down as a departure from the gospels. Seen historically, the Christian culture of the West has as its foundation the alliance of Church and State under the *Sacrum Imperium*. It is, however, necessary to bear in mind the psychological after-effects of medieval clericalism which persist even now and to derive our theo-

[3] St. Gregory of Nazianzus, *Oration over Basil the Great:* Migne PG 36, 508 ff.

logical orientation from the apostolic idea of the Church. The functions of the general priesthood, therefore, can and should be considered in the context of its exemplar and source, Christ the High Priest of the New Covenant.

The teaching function consists for the laity in the general bearing of witness to Christ and the kingdom of God on earth. It is most in evidence, for example, in the instruction which the father and mother of the Christian family give to their children and this is of course far more important than the religious instruction given by priests. It is also expressed in lay co-operation in the work of the apostles and we are given a vivid picture of this in the final chapter of the Epistle to the Romans where Paul commends "Phoebe . . . she has devoted her services to the church at Cenchrae . . ., and sends greetings to Prisca and Aquila, who have worked at my side in the service of Jesus Christ . . . and to Mary, who has spent so much labour on you . . . to Andronicus and Junias, kinsmen and fellow-prisoners of mine, who have won repute among the apostles that were in Christ's service before me . . . to Urbanus, who helped our work in Christ's cause . . . and to Apelles, a man tried in Christ's service" (Rom. 16:1–10).

From such evidence it is clear that the laity was not considered in a purely passive capacity as the object of the preaching of the Word. The "hearing" Church is not to be distinguished from the "teaching" Church as being merely receptive, for all adult baptized Christians are on principle committed actively to bear witness to the Church and their vital function is to preserve the treasure of revelation. In his famous essay "On Consulting the Faithful in Matters of Doctrine" (1859) Newman gave a concrete example of the collaboration of the laity in the preservation of doctrine. In the critical doctrinal disputes about Arianism in the fourth and fifth centuries it was the lay people and the minor clergy who saved the faith when it was attacked by the power of the Byzantine state. The majority of the episcopate, with some famous exceptions like Athanasius, Gregory of Nazianzus, Gregory of Nyssa, Basil and Chrysostom, gave in to state pressure. God's promise of support for his whole Church held good in this critical situation in spite of the defection of an important part of the Church.

In this context too it is worthwhile remembering the rôle of the laity in the great Councils, for the emperors were represented by their legates up till the time of Trent and wielded varying degrees of influence, usually on the side of peace and moderation.

The priestly function of the laity – "priestly" here being understood in the specific sense of a part-function besides teaching and spiritual discipline – can be seen as much in the administration of sacraments as in pastoral work. The power of baptism is not a privilege of the priest; the sacramental bond of matrimony is bestowed by the married couple on one another. They mirror the love of Christ for his redeemed Church (Eph. 5:22f.) and sanctify themselves and their children. Paul even maintains that the child of Christian parents receives a certain sanctification, an objective relationship with the kingdom of God, before baptism and that this is due to his being born of sanctified parents, even if only one of them is a believer (1 Cor. 7:14).

Peter too speaks in the passage already cited of the ability and vocation of all Christians "to offer up that spiritual sacrifice which God accepts through Jesus Christ" and "to proclaim the exploits of the God who has called you out of darkness into his marvellous light". Spiritual sacrifices are the proofs of love through which a man sets aside his own self for God's sake; through them the baptized Christian is consciously or unconsciously included in the one sacrifice. He is also incorporated in it through his sacramental co-operation, when he participates with the community in the celebration of the Eucharist; as the liturgy says, "we, thy servants, as also thy holy people" offer it up in Christ so that "my sacrifice and your sacrifice" – the priest is enacting the liturgy with the people – "may be acceptable to God the Father almighty".

It is true that the actual consecration is reserved to priests, but through the mystical and spiritual priesthood of all believers the unbloody sacrifice of the mediator becomes the sacrifice of the totality of the faithful.[4] At a time when the understanding of the celebration of the Eucharist as the communal act of all the faithful in Christ threatened to disappear and the so-called private Masses in monasteries made the sacred act seem almost a kind of

---

[4] Geiselmann, *Die theologische Anthropologie J. A. Möhlers* (1955), p. 52; cf. Möhler, *Einheit* (1952), pp. 251 ff.

personal devotion for the priest, we find the theologian St. Peter Damian (1006-72 A.D.) speaking out in the spirit of the early Church on the union of priest and people in the holy Sacrifice: "The Church of Christ is inwardly so fused in unity by the bond of mutual love that through the sacramental mystery she is one in many and yet whole in each individual. This is true to such an extent that on the one hand the whole Church is rightly designated 'the one bride of Christ' and yet according to our faith and by reason of the sacramental mystery each individual is the embodiment of the Church in all her richness . . . . She is made one and simple from many through union of faith, and made many from individuals through unifying love and the various gifts of the Spirit, because all originate in the one. . . . According to the rule of church tradition, whatever any member of the Church does reverently in the sacred liturgy is also efficacious for the common faith and devotion of all. For the Spirit of the Church is one and he inspires the one body which owes its continuing existence to Christ the head: 'You are one body, with a single Spirit; each of you, when he was called, called in the same hope' (Eph. 4:4). This explains the words in the celebration of Mass: 'For them do we offer or they do themselves offer up to thee this sacrifice of praise.' From these words it is quite evident that the sacrifice of praise is offered by all the faithful together, not only by men but by the women too, although it seems that the priest is especially elevated and that seemingly he alone offers the sacrifice. For what he holds in his hands to offer up to God, is in fact being offered by the whole multitude of the faithful in the collective surrender of their hearts."[5]

Moreover, all participate, to the extent of their interior adherence to Christ and their particular gifts of grace, through their prayers and intercessions in the building of holy Church and of God's kingdom on earth. As Cardinal Newman points out in one of his sermons, it is the royal privilege of all the faithful to pray not only for themselves but also as intercessors for others in association with the great High Priest and mediator: "(Intercession), I say, is the Christian's especial prerogative; and if he does not exercise it, certainly he has not risen to the conception of his real place among created beings . . . . Viewed in himself he ever prays for pardon and confesses sin; but viewed in Christ, he 'has access unto this grace wherein we stand, and rejoices in hope of the glory of God' (Rom. 5:2). Viewed in his place in 'the Church of the First-born enrolled in heaven', with his original debt cancelled in baptism . . . clad in the garments of righteousness, anointed with oil, and with a crown upon his head, in royal and priestly garb, as an heir of eternity . . . such a one, I repeat it, is plainly in his fitting place when he intercedes. He is made after the pattern and in the fulness of Christ – he is what Christ is. Christ intercedes above, and he intercedes below."[6] St. Theresa of the Child Jesus too felt deeply that this was so, as one of her letters shows: "So incomprehensible, so tender is Jesus'

---

[5] "On the *Dominus vobiscum*" 5, 7, 8: Migne PL 145, 235 ff.
[6] *Parochial and Plain Sermons* III, 24, pp. 362f.

love for us, that he wishes to do nothing unless we do it with him: we are to participate with him in the salvation of souls. The creator of the universe waits for the prayer and the devotion of one poor humble soul, in order to save many others who have also been redeemed by the price of his blood. Is not the apostolic service of prayer, dare I say so, not more sublime even than the service of the word?"[7]

To a certain extent the general priesthood has a part also in the power of forgiving sins which Christ left to his Church: first of all by our making amends mutually and forgiving one another, which has power in heaven as is presupposed in the passage of St. James (5:16), and expounded by the great theologians of the Church;[8] also through the community in the sacramental discipline of the Church, as we find it in Paul's letters (1 Cor. 5; 2 Cor. 2) and as J. A. Jungmann has shown in his study of the ancient liturgy of the Mass, where the people co-operate in the reconciliation of sinners to the Church in the "Prayers for penitents", still retained today as the *Preces super populum* in Lent.

Co-operation in prayer is to be supplemented by fraternal admonishing. What is meant by this may be shown by one of the early Fathers, St. John Chrysostom, who in his popular homilies on the Bible wrote: "In such a state of mind (that of salutary zeal) should we sorrow with the priests over the sinners; for it does not all depend on them, much depends on us too. For instance, if the sinner sees that he is rebuked by the father yet held in affection

---

[7] To her sister Céline, 12: *Letters*.
[8] Origen, *De Or.* 28, 19; Augustine, *Sermones* 82, 7; *In Joh.* 58, 5.

by his brothers and sisters, he does not take it so hard. If then the father administers a reproof, you should join in his anger.... Otherwise you pull down what I am building up – and what do we achieve but the aggravation of the trouble? In addition, you bring down on your own head not only harm but even punishment; for any man who hinders the healing of the wound has not a lesser but a greater punishment than the original sinner."[9]

It is clear that here, as in the biblical sources, in addition to communal prayer for penitents, fraternal reproofs, in some circumstances even disassociation from those in error, is stressed as an expression of the responsibility of all the members of the Church for one another. In other words, included in the mission of the priestly people is a participation in the pastoral office, in the spiritual power of order and discipline in the Church. According to biblical and early Christian tradition this is shown in many ways: When Paul admonishes parents with regard to their children: "The training, the discipline in which you bring them up must come from the Lord" (Eph. 6:4), he is implying a participation in the priestly power of the one Shepherd of the Church. And when Christ himself praises brotherly admonition as a duty of love (Matt. 18:15 ff.) and John demands that the Church refuse welcome to those who persist in error (2 John 10), these are manifestations in practice of the power which in more recent times Pius XI described as "the participation of all the faithful in the hierarchical apostolate".

[9] *In Cor. hom.* 14, 3: Migne PG 61, 500.

On good grounds, Karl Rahner[10] has referred to a gap in
present canon law, as far as the powers of the general
priesthood are concerned. The disputes between the
hierarchy and the Emperor during the Middle Ages meant
that the privileges of the clergy were fought for and written down in canon law. But the right of the laity to consultation in the matters affecting the kingdom of God is
only rarely in evidence. It is true that when the banns of
marriage are called and at the ordination of priests,
everyone is required to use his responsibility for the community by raising his objections if he has any. For the
most part, however, the rights and duties of the laity in
canon law have remained unexplored – a striking negligence, in contrast with the innumerable articles of the
code dealing with the clergy. "We shall be waiting in
vain for Catholic Action to become genuine and direct
collaboration with the clergy as long as the layman in
Catholic Action has merely to carry out someone else's
will, be it that of priest or bishop, without any independence, and as long as there are no proper rights for the
laity in Catholic Action, protecting their position also
vis à vis the hierarchy." Naturally such legislation will
be ineffective unless the spirit of religious education aims
at the free personal responsibility of Christians, unless
priests engaged in education take to heart the principle
of Pius XI: "It is essential so to form the consciences of
the faithful that at all times and in all situations both of
public and private life they are capable of finding for

---

[10] *Theological Investigations* II (Eng. tr. 1963).

148

themselves the Christian solutions of the many problems they encounter."

The relationship between the general priesthood and the special priesthood can be explained in many ways. What is certain from the early apostolic and biblical tradition is that the official priesthood is handed on by means of a special laying-on of hands of sacramental character, because of its special responsibility and with regard to particular spiritual powers. We notice this as early as the consecration of the seven (Acts 6:6) and at the consecration of the presbyter-bishops (Acts 14:22) and in the pastoral letters (1 Tim. 2:14; 2 Tim. 1:7). The question of exactly what relationship exists between the general and the special priesthood is, however, a relatively subordinate one in theological discussion.

Generally, according to scholastic theology, the priesthood of Jesus was held to flow from the apostles to their consecrated successors in office, in whose dignity and mission the lower orders of the priesthood (deacons and other assistants down to the general priesthood of all the faithful) had a share. The Fathers of the Church and contemporary theologians, however, explain the universal Church of the "priestly nation" as Christ's "bride" in the Holy Spirit and as the fruitful mother of all the effects of salvation including the powers of consecration and blessing in the Church. Augustine, in particular, puts forward this view in his doctrine against Donatism: *Gratia per Christum in ecclesia.*[11] Although no one is holy

---

[11] Augustine, *Ep.* 140, 3.

in the full meaning of the word, all the baptized are
children of the blessed Mother, members of the mystical
Body in the Holy Ghost. In St. Augustine's image, it is the
"dove" inspired by the Spirit which baptizes and consecrates, forgives sins and gives blessings – in the name of
the High Priest, Christ – and those who are consecrating
are only instruments, channels, "midwives" and not
"mothers" of the supernatural life.[12] Holy Mother Church,
the priestly nation, the communion of saints makes
decisions out of her deposit of faith through the bishops
and under the guidance of the Chair of Peter, *quod uni-
versae placuit Ecclesiae,*[13] and by virtue of her authority in
the Holy Spirit makes use of those who have been ordained
to forgive sins, to consecrate and to bless. Sinners too belong
to the Church as a visible body; but as the communion
of grace, as "bride", as the communion of saints, as
"dove", it is through her that grace is actually bestowed.
In a summary of St. Augustine's views on the relationship
between the official and the general priesthood it is
stated:[14] "The Church is in truth 'mother' only in her
saints; for in these and in these only is inherent the life-
creating force through the Holy Spirit, who lives in them;
the imparting of the forgiveness of sins and of new life
is part of that mystical and vital function which takes
place between the saints and those sinners who come to

[12] Augustine, *Contra Pet.* 3, 54; 66; *Ep.* 98, 5; *De bapt.* 2, 18, 23;
Morin, *S. Aug. Sermones* (1930), pp. 371 ff. etc.
[13] Augustine, *Contra Cresc.* 1, 33.
[14] F. Hofmann, *Der Kirchenbegriff des hl. Augustinus* (1933), pp. 274 f.

the Church with the disposition of inner charity and as such it is not a privilege of the ecclesiastical officialdom; rather the official priest is involved in this vital spiritual interchange not as *minister* but as *sanctus* .... The distinction between clergy and laity exists only in the sphere of the visible Church and there plays an important rôle; in the sphere of the invisible Church it has no place. Here all the 'saints' (all those made holy), whether clergy or laity, form one 'royal priesthood' whose task it is to obtain for others, in the way laid down by Christ, union with the sublime and true High Priest, with whom they themselves are united .... It would be true to say that in his teaching on 'holy Mother Church' Augustine grasped and developed more profoundly than ever before or since the fundamental idea of the Catholic priesthood of the laity, as it issued from the doctrine of the Church as the Body of Christ." Newman's ideas on this subject echo those of St. Augustine when he suggests that, while the visible order of powers in the Church recognizes different degrees of participation in the authority of Christ, the saints are the real representatives of the Church.[15]

It is the historical defect of the Reformation that it disparaged or even denied the importance of the official priesthood in favour of the general priesthood, without any real benefit to the latter. The Counter-Reformation was tempted to disparage the general priesthood in favour of the hierarchical priesthood – and it cannot be denied that this defect too had damaging results. If then we hope

[15] *Parochial and Plain Sermons* III, pp. 220 ff., 236 ff.

that Protestant Christians will give real consideration to the importance and function of the office of priest, we too must make our contribution towards bringing back and translating into real terms the early Church's religious awareness, as we see it in the New Testament, of the responsibility of all Christians to bear witness to Christ.

The Communion of Saints

THE NINTH article of the Apostles' Creed can be taken to mean either the communion in saintliness or the communion of saints; for the words used in the Greek and Latin leave open both interpretations, that is, whether the common participation of all in the goods of salvation is meant or the personal communion of saints (those who have been sanctified) among themselves. The context – *sanctorum communio* is followed by "the forgiveness of sins" – would seem to point more to the first meaning: the participation of all in saintliness. And we frequently find the words "communion" or "fellowship" or "common participation" used in Scripture in this sense: "The God, who has called you into the fellowship of his Son, Jesus Christ our Lord, is faithful to his promise" (1 Cor. 1:9). "Is not this cup we bless a participation in Christ's blood? Is not the bread we break a participation in Christ's body?" (1 Cor. 10:16.) Similarly: "The grace of our Lord Jesus Christ, and the love of God, and the imparting of (*i. e.* communion in) the Holy Spirit be with you all"

(2 Cor. 13:13). Through our faith in Christ we learn "what it means to share his sufferings" (Phil. 3:10), that is, to participate in the blessings of the redemption by virtue of his cross. All these different expressions are referring to *communio* in the sense of a participation in Christ, in the Holy Spirit, in the merits of salvation.

The particular occasion on which our consciousness of this participation is renewed and deepened is the communal celebration of the Eucharist. Here, as in all the sacraments, the participation of all in Christ is real – just as baptism makes us members of the Body of Christ, so "we too, all of us, have been baptized into a single body by the power of a single Spirit" (1 Cor. 12:13) – and we celebrate in the Eucharist the mystery of the union of all those at the table in Christ: "The one bread makes us one body, though we are many in number; the same bread is shared by all" (1 Cor. 10:17). The sacrament of penance too, as is particularly clear in its early Christian form, is the transition from exclusion from the sacramental communion to re-acceptance into the *communio in ecclesia.*

From the consciousness of communion in holiness there arose quite naturally the other concept, the communion of all the participants with one another. Through the common reception of the gifts of salvation, that is, the communion of the children of God sealed by baptism, those who had been sanctified recognized one another as belonging together, "as the one holy Church, the communion of saints"; out of this experience of communion in spiritual goods there was established the consciousness of

154

brotherhood, characterized by love.[1] From about the fourth century this second sense of the communion of saints took precedence and it was in this sense that it was understood by the Gallic bishops who inserted the article into the Apostles' Creed, since its content had always been part of the faith. It was not long before a further meaning was attached to this stressing of the reciprocal personal relationship: a particular predilection arose for associating it with the bond between the earthly and the heavenly Church, the communion of the faithful with the blessed in heaven. There is no doubt that this idea too has its foundation in the apostolic faith, for "the scene of your approach now is Mount Sion, is the heavenly Jerusalem, city of the living God; here are gathered thousands upon thousands of angels, here is the assembly of those first-born sons whose names are written in heaven" (Heb. 12:22, 23). Nonetheless, a certain shift of emphasis in the approach and in the religious interest of the faithful can be perceived: whereas originally "the saints" are all those who have been sanctified – all the faithful who through baptism and their life of faith show forth the

---

[1] For the historical development of the concept from the sense of "participation in what is holy" to "communion of the saints" see the following: J. A. Jungmann in *Zeitschrift für katholische Theologie* (1962), pp. 212ff.; H. de Lubac, *Corpus mysticum* (1944); J. R. Geiselmann, *Die theologische Anthropologie J. A. Möhlers* (1955), pp. 56ff. – In agreement with the above are the Protestant studies: E. Wolf, *Sanctorum communio in Peregrinatio* (1954); W. Elert, *Abendmahl und Kirchengemeinschaft in der alten Kirche* (1955).

mystical Christ – now moral perfection is particularly stressed. Since the Middle Ages the word "saint" has implied those men and women of exemplary conduct who have now received "the crown of life" and who act as intercessors in heaven for those still on earth.

The main ideas which led to this development and form the basis for the veneration of the saints are as follows:

1. All those who belong to Christ are sanctified through the mystical yet real communion with the Creator, the one Holy One, for "all completeness dwells in him" (Col. 1:19). All the sanctified are branches of the one vine on which they "yield abundant fruit" (John 15:5). "You have only to live on me and I will live in you", Jesus said of them (John 15:4); "if anyone does the will of God he is my brother, and sister, and mother" (Mark 3:35). Therefore "you are all brethren alike" (Matt. 23:8) and should see him in everyone and welcome even little children as the Lord did (Matt. 9:35f.).

2. The communion of the sanctified, the mystical Body of the Lord, embraces both this world and the next. We see that "angels came and ministered" (Matt. 4:11) to the Lord in his earthly life and encouraged him (Luke 22:43) and that the great mediators of the Old Law appeared beside him at the transfiguration on the mountain, as a sign that he would not stand alone in the imminent struggle. The faithful too know that they have not been abandoned in the earthly fight: "Here are the spirits of just men, now made perfect; here is Jesus the spokesman of the New Covenant" (Heb. 12:24). In other words

the heavenly communion is one with the Church on earth and there is no separation between them. It is to "our mother the heavenly Jerusalem" (Gal. 4:26) that St. Paul refers the Galatians in their difficulties, for "we find our true home in heaven. It is to heaven that we look expectantly for the coming of our Lord Jesus Christ to save us" (Phil. 3:20). Already God "has raised Christ Jesus. He would have all future ages see, in that clemency which he showed us in Christ Jesus, the surpassing richness of his grace" (Eph. 2:6).

3. The faithful on earth and the blessed in heaven are united with one another by a spiritual bond of love and prayers. The people on earth are also joined to one another in this way, just as they are joined to the blessed in heaven, in the *one* communion of saints.

There is only one High Priest who "lives on still to make intercession on our behalf" (Heb. 7:25), but in him the "Head" in whom "all subsist" (Col. 1:17), all the faithful are qualified for and consecrated to a holy, royal priesthood, "to offer up that spiritual sacrifice which God accepts through Jesus Christ" (1 Pet. 2:5). Just as the divine power of creation in no way excludes the powers of nature but enables these powers to be fruitful, so the High Priest of salvation does not exclude the priesthood of the sanctified believers, but gives it power in his name; and "you have only to make any request of the Father in my name, and he will grant it to you" (John 16:23).

As early as Old Testament times we see Abraham pleading with God for Sodom threatened by divine judgment

157

and being told that if even ten just men could be found there, God would spare it (Gen. 18:23ff.). The Patriarchs speak a blessing over the generations to come; Moses repeatedly intercedes for his sinful people, even offering himself as a pledge: "I entreat thee, pardon this offence of theirs; or else blot out my name too from the record thou hast written" (Exod. 32:32). It is to his prayers on the mountain that the people owe their victory over the Amalecites (Exod. 17:8). It is said of Job: "as Job prayed for these friends of his, the Lord relented at the sight of his penitence" (Job 42:10). In the gospels Jesus often lets himself be moved by intercessors to give proofs of his love to those in distress. So Mary puts in her plea at the wedding for the bridal couple and her plea is not in vain (John 2). So the centurion pleads on behalf of his servant and is not only heard but praised too for his great faith (Matt. 8). So Jesus heals the man sick of the palsy at the silent request of his friends and gives him, moreover, health of soul (Matt. 9). On the cross he himself prays for his persecutors (Luke 23:34), as he had admonished his disciples to do: "Love your enemies . . . pray for those who persecute and insult you" (Matt. 5:44). Even more he prays for his friends, given to him by the Father; the Our Father is the prayer of all for one another: "Give us this day our daily bread, forgive us our trespasses . . . deliver us from evil" (Matt. 6:11f.). Paul asks the Romans: "Only, brethren, I entreat you by our Lord Jesus Christ, and by the love of the Holy Spirit, to give me the help of your prayers to God on my behalf" (Rom. 15:30). To the Corinthians he writes that God "has preserved us, and is

158

preserving us from such deadly peril.... Only you too must help us with your prayers" (2 Cor. 1:10). He urges his disciple Timothy "that petition, prayer, entreaty and thanksgiving should be offered for all mankind . . . it is what God, our Saviour, expects of us, since it is his will that all men should be saved" (1 Tim. 2:1–4). He himself assures the churches that he has them continually in his prayers (Col. 1:3). His blessings are prayers of love: "The grace of our Lord Jesus Christ be with you; and my love be with you all in Christ Jesus" (1 Cor. 16:23). And his relationship with the churches is given clear expression by these endings of his epistles: "Brethren, pray for us.... The grace of our Lord Jesus Christ be with you" (Thess. 5:25–28) or "Here is a greeting for you from Paul in his own hand; do not forget that he is a prisoner. Grace be with you" (Col. 4:18).

With his prayers of intercession the apostle offers up too his toils and sorrows for the faithful: "Even as I write, I am glad of my sufferings on your behalf, as, in this mortal frame of mine, I help to pay off the debt which the afflictions of Christ still leave to be paid, for the sake of his body, the Church" (Col. 1:24). His confidence and trust come not so much from the fact that he himself has behaved "with single-heartedness and sincerity in God's sight" (2 Cor. 1:12), for he asks himself, "What powers hast thou, that did not come to thee by gift?" (1 Cor. 4:7), but because "it is Christ that lives in me" (Gal. 2:20) and "Christ Jesus has won the mastery over me" (Phil. 3:12). From here the perspective leads clearly to what might be called the co-operation of the creature in salvation: the importance of the general priesthood lies above all in the prayers of intercession and the conciliatory sacrifices of the sanctified. It must be added here that the same basic ideas run through the writings of the other apostolic witnesses (Jas. 5:16; 1 John 5:16).

There are many references in the New Testament to justify the assumption of a relationship between those in heaven and those on earth. We have already mentioned the angels during the earthly life of Christ. Mary, Joseph and Zachary too receive their revelations of God's will from angels. Jesus says that there is joy before the angels when one sinner does penance (Luke 15:7–11). It may be taken as mere traditional embroidering of the parable that the rich man expresses a wish to warn his brethren with a message from beyond the grave – through Abraham's help, for his own connection with the earth has been broken – but the Lord's admonition is clear: "Make use of your base wealth to win yourselves friends, who, when you leave it behind will welcome you into eternal habitations" (Luke 16:9). The prayers of our friends interceding for us can help us into the next life. The twenty-four elders in the Apocalypse, the representatives of the earthly communion, bear "golden bowls full of incense, the prayers of the saints" (Apoc. 5:8) that is, the prayers of the faithful on earth which they offer to God: they are thus giving their support to the prayers of those on earth; and "the souls of all those who had been slain for love of God's word" (Apoc. 6:9) also pray that their earthly brothers may have patience in tribulation and be redeemed from affliction. There is a connecting link between these

160

New Testament examples and early Christian invocations, for instance those of the Christians in the catacomb of St. Sebastian in Rome, where another martyr for Christ is commemorated in artless scrawls on the wall: *Sancte Petre, ora pro nobis;* or the blessings for the departed on their gravestones: *Pax, lux, refrigerium* (peace, light, and refreshment), words which are still retained today in the prayers for the dead in the liturgy of the Mass.

4. In Scripture too the perfect saints are held up as models for our own sanctification. There is one above all on whom we should "fix our eyes", Jesus, "the origin and the crown of all faith" (Heb. 12:2), but those who imitate him share in his perfection. Here we are dealing with something other than an example in a worldly sense, for the sake of human character and human achievements. For what is human "sanctity"? Even Paul, who can presume to put himself forward to the Philippians as an example to be imitated, is conscious all the time that he cannot claim "any justification that is my own work, given me by the law, but the justification that comes from believing in Jesus Christ, God's gift on condition of our faith" (Phil. 3:9). But, granted this, there is according to Scripture a process of growth and perfection in the heavenly gifts we have received and the degree of this perfection is dependent also on personal readiness and devotion. According to Paul, not all the members of the Body of Christ have the same "honour" (1 Cor. 12:24); from Christ each limb "receives the active power it needs" (Eph. 4:16). In the temple of God, the foundation of which is Jesus Christ, "different men will build in gold, silver, precious

161

stones, wood, grass or straw, and each man's workmanship will be plainly seen" (1 Cor. 3:12f.). According to whether the scattered seed of the kingdom of God is preserved by those "with a noble and generous heart" or whether it is "stifled by the cares, the riches, and the pleasures of life", so that the fruit "never reaches maturity" (Luke 8:14f.), the seed yields "a harvest, some a hundredfold, some sixtyfold, some thirtyfold" or else is ruined from the very beginning (Matt. 13:8–23). According to how a man deals with the talents entrusted to him, will he receive either more or less (Matt. 25:14ff.). The innumerable admonitions of the apostles are derived from their view of a graduated sanctity according to God's free choice when bestowing his grace (Rom. 19:14ff.), but at the same time this is in proportion to a man's devotion, through which faith becomes active in love. The kingdom of heaven is depicted in the image of a feast at which some sit far below and others high up (Luke 14:10ff.); and the apostles, who "have forsaken all" to follow the Lord, "shall sit on twelve thrones ... and shall be judges over the twelve tribes of Israel", but "many will be first that were last, and last that were first" (Matt. 19:28ff.).

Any teacher knows of the importance of an inspiring example and the Bible confirms this. The way in which in the Old Testament Abraham the Father is shown as the champion of faith suggests the sense of elevation and encouragement of religious endeavour[2]. The urgent

---

[2] 1 Esdras 9:7; Judith 8:22; Ecclus. 44:20; Isa. 44:8; Dan. 3:35; 1 Mach. 2:52.

cry in Machabees is a striking example: "Your fathers, what deeds they did in their time! Great glory would you win and a deathless name, let these be your models. See how Abraham was tested, and how trustfulness of his was counted virtue in him; see how Joseph in ill fortune was true to the commandment still, and came to be ruler of all Egypt" (1 Mach. 2:51). Then Elias is cited and Ananias, Azarias and Misael, who overcame the furnace, and god-fearing Daniel and finally comes the exhortation: "Nay, my sons, take courage; in the law's cause rally you, in the law's annals you shall win renown" (2 Mach. 2:64). In the book of Ecclesiasticus, which is often quoted in the New Testament, veneration of the heroes of religion seems to be one of the author's main concerns: "Speak we now in honour of famous men . . . . What high achievements the Lord has made known in them, ever since time began! . . . Their wisdom is yet a legend among the people; wherever faithful men assemble, their story is told" (Ecclus. 44:1 ff.). It is, in fact, an echo of the psalms: "Right reason is on the good man's lips . . . his steps never falter" (Ps. 36:30). "The innocent man will flourish as the palm-tree flourishes. . . . Planted in the temple of the Lord, growing up in the very courts of our God's house . . . " (Ps. 91:13f.). For "dear in the Lord's sight is the death of those who love him . . . Lord . . . . Thou hast broken the chains that bound me; I will sacrifice in thy honour, and call upon the name of the Lord" (Ps. 115:6f.).

That the men of the New Testament thought similarly is shown by the epistle to the Hebrews, where all through two chapters the great spiritual leaders of old are held up

163

THE KINGDOM OF GOD TODAY

as examples to the faithful (Heb. 11–12). And above all it is
the mother of Jesus whom the apostles commemorate
with exceptional respect; it was probably after the Assumption when the apostles spoke of her, mentioning the prophecy that she, "the handmaid of the Lord", would be
called blessed by all the generations to come (Luke 1:48).
Before he parted from them, Jesus had told his closest
friends that "after a little while" they would see him again
(John 16:16) and later he adds, praying to his Father: "And
I have given them the privilege which thou gavest to me ....
So let the world know that it is thou who hast sent me, and
that thou hast bestowed thy love upon them" (John 17:
22f.). It is a fact, attested by early Christian writers, that
Peter and Paul, for example, were honoured as the heroes
and martyrs of religion;[3] the general honour accorded to
those who died for Christ in the early Christian eras can be
judged from the letters of St. Ignatius of Antioch, who was
greeted by the churches on his journey to martyrdom
about 107 A.D., and a generation later about 156 A.D. from
Polycarp's greatly venerated martyrdom: "That was
Polycarp, the wonderful martyr among the elect. He was
throughout his life an apostle and prophet to our age,
the bishop of the Catholic Church in Smyrna. . . . Christ
alone can we worship, but to the martyrs we show that
love, which is due to them as disciples and followers of the
Lord for their unsurpassable devotion to the King and
Master. . . . In celebrating his memory we remember all

[3] 1 Clement 5:4ff.; Dionysius of Corinth, *To the Romans* (in Eu-
sebius 2:25); Irenaeus, *Adv. haer.* III, 1; 4, 3.

who have already fought the fight and we pray for the strengthening and preparing of those who have still to engage upon it."

Everywhere the veneration of the saints has grown and enriched the piety of Christian people. In comparison with popular piety and its invocations of the saints for all kinds of special requests and intentions, their liturgical veneration in the Mass is very simple and is limited in most cases to the basic form of prayer: "Grant us, o Lord, through their intercession, that we too may live according to their example" or similar words. As far as popular Catholic customs and ways of venerating the saints are concerned, there may in good faith be many different opinions. There is, however, no doubt that essentially this veneration is in accordance with the spirit of the Bible: to honour "the divine mystery and the holiness of man."[4] Just as "the skies proclaim God's glory" (Ps. 18:1), so the saints are, as Newman said, the glad and complete specimens of the new creation which our Lord brought into the moral world. For ordinary people theology is often less accessible than the language of images and examples from life itself, and herein lies the importance of biographies of the saints: their development, their inner struggles, and their perfection have the attraction of living reality for everyone. Significantly enough, Newman's own experience was that nothing was more elevating for the mind than the consciousness of being one of a great and victorious communion. He points out, too, that "the divine origin of

---

[4] Franz Werfel in his preface to *The Song of Bernadette*.

Christianity is shown not in its marked effects on the mass of mankind, but in its surprising power of elevating the moral character where it is received in spirit and in truth. Its scattered saints, in all ranks of life, speak of it to the thoughtful inquirer".[5] "They are witnesses for God and Christ, in their lives and by their protestations, without judging others, or exalting themselves . . . . They are witnesses, as light witnesses against dark by the contrast – giving good and receiving back evil." So it is that religious men find in the saints that spiritual strength and "consolation to support them, which the Visible Church seems, at first sight, not to supply, when the overflowings of ungodliness make them afraid."[6]

[5] Newman, *Oxford University Sermons* III, p. 41.
[6] Newman, *Parochial and Plain Sermons* III, 17, p. 242.

The Kingdom of God —
Borne by His People

As THE nursery of the religious spirit in man the Church
will always present a contrast to earthly forms of civilization; religious and secular education will always remain
distinct. This early resulted, as far as the clergy were concerned – that is, those set apart for the official service of the
Church – in a special form of spiritual education. Separate
institutions were created for theology and spirituality;
there was the liturgical separation of the choir, reserved
for the clergy, from the nave, reserved for the people;
different religious vestments and (in the Latin Church)
the law of the celibate life increased the gulf between
priests and people. The religious element became so
emphatically and exclusively the very centre of the
Church's spirituality, that a certain psychological alienation inevitably occurred between clergy and laity.

And yet the laity belong equally with the clergy to the
union which is the Church and secular cultural spheres
belong to the kingdom of God as much as spiritual and
religious values. The sacramental actions of the priest,

his service of the word of God and the sacraments and the layman's work in his innumerable secular duties, from unskilled labour to scientific research and to art, belong each in the same degree to the world of God. Everything "whether it be . . . the world, or life, or death, or the present, or the future, it is all for you, and you for Christ, and Christ for God" (1 Cor. 3:22). "In eating, in drinking, in all that you do, do everything as for God's glory" (1 Cor. 10:31). For Christians any fundamental distinction between the religious and the profane is impossible: there is nothing in God's creation which has not been designed to show forth his glory.

In his own earthly life Christ united man's two functions, the sacral and the profane. He was true man, body and soul. For the greater part of his life he was "the carpenter's son" and it was only for about a tenth of his earthly existence that he undertook the vocation in which he is the model for all those who serve in the Church. Consequently in the kingdom of God religion cannot place itself in opposition to the secular vocation, nor can the latter oppose itself to religion. A man's spiritual and secular vocations are interdependent and only have their full value in a union in which they complement one another (1 Cor. 12). In the course of history, however, the general tendency for the education of priests to be kept isolated from the world – in the Latin countries segregation began even in boyhood – led to a corresponding spiritual alienation on both sides, which could only with difficulty be overcome by exceptional priestly love and which, in fact, was often characterized by mutual mistrust, if nothing worse.

Is this inevitable? If we take the life of Christ as our model it should be possible to find a proper relationship. Just as Christ, when he was a craftsman and carpenter in Nazareth, belonged to God as much as when he went out as a preacher or when he died for many on the cross, so equally in the Christian view of life the earthly profession of the layman is no less pleasing to God than the function of the priest. The general priesthood with its witness to the kingdom of God, with its authority to educate the family, with its living participation in the sacred sacrifice and with what Pius XI called the "co-operation in the hierarchical apostolate of the Church", has its roots in a real sharing in the royal and priestly dignity of Christ and should show itself, according to the individual's personal aptitude and inner desire, in the pursuance of the Christian mission in the world. In both states – that of the priest as that of the layman – man can reach an equal degree of perfection in and through faith, love, and obedience to God's will, just as in both he can remain imperfect, even to the extent of complete failure. Religion demands from the individual a devotion to the kingdom of God and complete trust in his grace amid all human shortcomings. The essence of piety, according to St. James, is to be found in practical works of charity and in keeping the heart untainted by evil. In general the laity will be both less suited and less inclined to the devotional life, which is completely understandable in the light of their vocation; and the clergy will in general have less aptitude and inclination for the secular spheres of culture, which is right for them. However, both should be aware of their limitations and cultivate mutual respect, serving one another as members of the same body. Conscious of his own struggle due to his "mixed" profession, as servant of both State and Church, Augustine wrote to the contemplative monks of Abbot Eudoxius: "When we think of the peace which you enjoy in Christ, it is for us, who are involved in many difficulties and outer adversities, a discovery of repose in your love: for are we not all one body under the one head? You stand with us in the forefront of our labours, we are with you in the silence of your meditation, for when one member suffers, all suffer with him and when one is in glory, all rejoice with him."

The life of Christ and the Pauline idea of the different gifts and offices in the one body of Christ teach us that in the final event the particular profession or particular type of vocational activity matters very little. The one thing of importance is the spirit, the disposition of love with which the individual performs any service whatever for the community. The "worldly piety" of the layman is in fact no less true devotion than is priestly piety, in spite of the fact the priest reserves certain hours each day for his devotions, while the layman usually has to content himself as far as pious exercises are concerned with Sunday Mass and the consecration of his daily work through his good intention. It is impossible to draw up standard regulations, the same for everyone.

How much the recognition of these facts means for a Christian evaluation of the ordinary aspects of every profession, for laying the foundation of a genuine self-confidence in the individual and for developing a consciousness of Christian dignity even in a supposedly "inferior" profession or way of life, has been shown, for example, by Yves Congar in his *Jalons pour une théologie du laïcat* (1953; Eng. tr. 1955). He rightly emphasizes the significance of the first article of the Creed: God the Creator as the basis of redemption and sanctification. The whole of creation has its source in God, the laws of nature are the expression of his eternal power and wisdom; the earth is given to man as the scene for him to develop his potentialities and capabilities; service to the community and work for the progress of human culture are holy, because they are the consummation of the divine mission. It would be a gross misunderstanding of the kingdom of God totally to divert the interest of the devout Christian from the things of this world to the things of the next and to equate Christian sanctity with escapism, with the denial of the natural values of love and marriage, of manual or intellectual work in the technical, economic, academic, artistic, or political spheres, and of the natural joys of life. The proclamation of the kingdom of God is concerned firstly and foremostly with this world: the rule of God is to be established here and now, as the "leaven" in the life of mankind which will mould the powers given to man by God for the good and inspire man's life with faith, hope, and charity to God and to his neighbour.

We are thus made aware of the function of a believing laity. The ministry of the Church can supply this laity only with spiritual food for its journey, enabling it to fulfil its function in the world in the spirit of Christ. This is what Clement of Alexandria did in describing for his age,

171

in his *Stromata,* the ideal of the Christian gnostic, of the wise man; nearer to our own time, St. Francis of Sales outlined his principles for piety in the world, principles which although still dominated by the rules of the priestly state were so advanced for his time that his viewpoint was far from being generally accepted or appreciated. Thus the secular spheres of culture separated themselves off from the influence of the Church, partly because the leading laymen felt themselves misunderstood in their best intentions, and on their side the clergy reacted with an even stricter segregration of their members from the profane world.

In addition, as is well known, there was the tragic social development of the last century which produced strained relations with the Church: the enormous social and economic changes which followed upon the industrial revolution went far ahead of the Church's pastoral care and confronted her with extremely difficult problems. The working classes, which were in fact the large majority of the people, were forced in almost every country into a position, in which they were dependent upon material and spiritual help. Many of them came to think that this help was to be gained most quickly and effectively from non-Christian socialism or even anti-religious communism, while ecclesiastical circles, perhaps for this very reason, were hesitant in their general attitude. Even after the popes had published their social teaching, there were relatively few priests who took it upon themselves to put this teaching into practice. It was not the good intentions which were lacking but rather a comprehensive and radical reorgani-

172

zation of pastoral methods, which would provide an approach on the spiritual level to the mass of people estranged from the Church. The priests cannot achieve this alone, although a sensible and determined distribution of forces could make up for a lot. One enormous handicap is the inflexibility due to the preservation of historical diocesan and parish boundaries with the result, particularly in traditional Catholic countries, that small villages often have a priest of their own while industrial centres and the suburbs have none or far too few. Above all, the principles of Catholic Action found little encouragement from the clergy themselves. These principles imply the formation of the laity for the sake of independent initiatives on the basis of their faith. In many countries this is the most challenging problem for the Church. The priest's resources are limited and unless the laity play their part, particularly among those classes to which the priest has difficulty of entry and approach, increasingly wider areas will be lost to the Church. Every communist is a pioneer – if only this were true, even to a small extent, of the members of the Church. It will only be possible if the clergy educate the most capable devout laymen as witnesses for Christ and send them out as independent, responsible and trusted co-workers. This should not involve any imposition of the priestly way of life on the inner circle of "lay apostles", and even less so on the average Christian in the world.

We cannot require of the pastor that he should put himself in the position of the technician or worker or father of a family, in order to share their way of life and literally to become "everything by turns to everybody", however

173

much we are moved by the generosity of the worker-priests. But the laity do have a right to expect that their position and importance for the kingdom of God should be honoured in the spirit of Christ and that a pastor should be able to sympathize with them in their situation with inner understanding and love. The Christian in the modern world is deeply and rightly convinced that his work in the various secular spheres of life can be, and when offered up for the community is, a means of giving true service to God.

It is true that there are jobs which a man naturally cannot really enjoy: jobs which make life very much like the existence of the slaves in ancient times. Yet there were many among them also who made St. Paul's words their own: "Yours must be a slavery of love, not to men, but to the Lord" (Eph. 6:7). In general, however, the job is automatically part of the man and therefore dear to him, whether it is in essence secular or spiritual: to a certain extent he is formed by it spiritually, since in the long run he cannot of himself change his way of life. He comes into contact with God and heaven less immediately in a secular vocation; he has to concern himself, at least mainly, with "things" and it is necessary for him if he wants to live and make progress to concentrate wholly on the aims of his work. Nonetheless, he feels that there is more to it, that as artisan, or technician or civil servant he is obeying a law that is not man-made: laws of nature scarcely suspected by science, laws of the conscience which a man finds within himself; and if he tries arbitrarily to set himself beyond these laws, he knows that it is the road to self-destruction. Through faith he becomes aware of the motivating forces which enable him to offer up his job and which make possible his whole mission in life: My work is my service; I work for my family and the work is in the final event for the purpose of helping the community of man, for the well-being of my brethren, of all those unknown to me. Active in my work is objective love, concrete love; and in bringing to the work the disposition of love, I sanctify it, I transform it into obedience to the plan of the Creator, who has commanded man to cultivate the earth and to make the forces of nature subject to him. The worker who year-in and year-out conscientiously goes through the same motions, the housewife who day after day cooks meals, sews, washes, irons, and cleans, giving up many of the enjoyments in life as a matter of course, are both performing faithfully a task which can be compared with the priest's, even though his task may intrinsically be higher. For it is not a man's exterior which makes him pure or impure, devout or not devout, pleasing to God or vile, but solely the attitude of mind with which he does what is his work in life (Matt. 15:11). It is not the intrinsic greatness of the work which determines a man's value, but the greatness of the love with which he serves God and his neighbour. This is what we must learn from Jesus the "man" and "the carpenter's son". He was no less pleasing to his heavenly Father in his humanity, while working in wood or stone and providing the people of Nazareth with his brotherly service, than serving the kingdom of God "directly" with his words and with his other sacrifice even to the acceptance of the bitter cup.

175

Good, competent workmanship primarily depends upon the character and disposition of the individual. The effort itself at first only indicates technical ability, but eventually needs to prove man's devotion to the task, his moral attitude and inspiration. He either serves society or stands aloof, declining his responsibility. Society determines the higher principles on which the kingdom of God is to be realized. It constitutes the common ground for the participation of all according to their calling, No calling is fundamentally inferior to another. All are of importance to the good of the whole. Each man's individual effort leads to the realization of God's kingdom on earth, including his unselfishness, his willingness to make a sacrifice and his love, which is as such identical with the love of the Divine. Whether man's immediate aim be towards material advancement, his inward consciousness will tell him: in serving society he is fulfilling a mission given him, not by man or any law of nature, but by the will of the Creator. And whatever he may do for the least of any of his brethren, he will do for him who became man, his brother incarnate, who has shared his afflictions and vicissitudes in common with us all. In forming himself upon Christ, his devotion will be acceptable to God. His work will in itself be his reward, and be it merely temporal, worldly, outwardly insignificant and not accomplishable without daily sacrifice on his part. His reward will be of the highest: of the love that sanctifies and will be his for all eternity.

The layman's job in life should, therefore, have the important function of maintaining in man's consciousness the bond between what is natural and earthly and what is divine and eternal. The world is God's creation and man has a divine purpose to fulfil in the world. Above us is God, beneath us nature, around us our fellow-men, before us the image of the Holy One, who came from God and became our true brother and remains so for all eternity.

We can never remind ourselves sufficiently how great and how incomparably important the model of Jesus' life on earth is for us. He spent the prime of his life in simple surroundings, in the humble work of a craftsman. But he brought to it just as much "soul" as to the final self-sacrifice which crowned his life. The divine purpose of his life lies not primarily in his dying but in his life itself, in the offering of his life in the service of his fellow-men, in his daily work, whether in the material or spiritual realm, for God makes no distinctions here. All-important is the fact that he practised what he preached: in his life he exemplified the love of man as worship of God, as the expression of love of God. Certainly he would even then have reserved a good part of his time for meditation on God's works and on the holy Scriptures of his people and given a greater degree of inspiration to his daily work with the prayers of his people, with the observances of the devout Jew. Even today the Oriental finds time more easily for his daily religious practices than the activist Westerner; prayer and work have a more obvious correlation for him than they have, or have ever had, for us in the West. But all this is of minor importance in comparison with what we must learn from his life among us: his life presents us with a model in which earthly service and piety do not exclude one another but are simply two aspects of our existence in the eyes of God: his work is prayer and his prayer an integral part of his work, because that work is a service rendered to his brothers. His love of the Father did not make him shun the things of earth, but rather find God in them. According to an uncanonical saying, which can be regarded as being genuine, he said: "Even when a person is alone, I am with him. Lift a stone and you will find me; chop the wood and I am there." In a similar vein he said of our relations with our fellow-men that "what ye do unto the least of these, my brethren, ye do unto me."

For a Christian life in the world we can then distinguish the following fundamentals:

1. Through his association in the communion of the Church – whether he is clearly conscious of it or not – the Christian receives his bond with Jesus Christ and with it his basic relationship to God, the surrender in faith to the Eternal Thou, and therefore the essential reason for love of his neighbour: "the faith that finds its expression in love is all that matters" (Gal. 5:6).

2. This essential association in the body of Christ, which is the Church, needs in addition a certain degree of religious practice in the narrow sense, which cannot be embodied in regulations in view of the very different requirements of individuals. In general, participation at Sunday Mass and Easter Communion (when necessary with confession beforehand) is the minimum. We are enjoined too to pray "in our inner room", that is, in the family, and to read the Holy Scriptures.

3. Moral endeavour consists in the main in the love of our neighbour, on a religious basis. It is in the sphere of his personal state, married or single, and of his profession that the individual fulfils his particular duty to the community and his personal worship of God. Everything else is left to the personal responsibility of the individual, to Christian freedom in the spirit of love. Everyone has his personal mission for the spiritual and temporal welfare of his fellow-men. In addition to his family and friends, contact with his pastors will be useful to him here too.

179

The Rule of God in Everyday Life

We are Christians through our bond with Jesus Christ, in our co-operation with his self-surrender to the Father in heaven and with his love of men. Wherever and whenever a man performs this act of faith, the intention of Jesus Christ is realized, the coming of the kingdom of God. And with this bond everything is renewed and we experience in a religious sense "eternal life" in its earthly beginnings.

The personal relationship between men is seen in a new light, as is the value of material possessions and the relationship between time and eternity. Some examples from the life of Christ may enliven our awareness of these truths:

1. In our relationship with our fellow-men, the giving of ourselves to the rule of God leads to a new spirit of brotherhood: "Thou shalt love the Lord thy God with thy whole heart and thy whole soul and thy whole mind. This is the greatest of the commandments, and the first. And the second, its like, is this, Thou shalt love thy neighbour as thyself. On these two commandments, all the law and the prophets depend" (Matt. 22:37–40).

180

Our neighbour is our brother because he is a man and because we both stand before God. It is as his brother that Jesus regards man and so he came himself as God's revelation, "the kindness of God, our Saviour, dawned on us, his great love for man" (Tit. 3:4). "Justice" is too little, love is the only bond.

Instead of laws and detailed regulations, Jesus left his disciples in the commandment of *caritas* one principle, one rule for all conceivable situations: "Do to other men all that you would have them do to you; that is the law and the prophets" (Matt. 7:12). An apocryphal variant runs: "You must not be glad until you have looked on your brother in love."

Every individual has his physical and spiritual talents, his education, his merits and defects, his responsibilities and sins; but he has too his vocation, his conscience, and the help of divine grace. No one has the right to judge others and if our neighbour falls into error, we should ask ourselves, as another traditional admonition of our Lord tells us, whether we do not also share his guilt: "If the neighbour of one of the elect (that is, one of the faithful) sins, then the elect too is guilty: for if he had lived as he should, the other would have been put to shame." This is a strong but profound expression of the union of all – as in Adam, so in Christ.

It is, however, their defects that we notice above all in our fellow-men, excepting our best friends. "All men are evil", says the man of the world with unconscious arrogance. "All men need God's mercy", should be the words of the believer.

It was precisely the sinners whom our Lord loved, that is, the men whom the judgment of the Pharisees characterized as such, the publicans, the harlots, and others. He stayed with Zacchaeus, he included the publican Matthew in his call; he defended the sinner, because he knew the greatness of the love she now had (Luke 7:47). No one should judge his fellow-man but should instead "be perfect as your heavenly Father is perfect", "who makes his sun rise on the evil and equally on the good, his rain fall on the just and equally on the unjust" (Matt. 5:45, 48).

Mercy includes readiness to forgive, not now and again, but "seventy times seven" that is, without counting at all. If we let God rule in us, our relationship with our fellow-men will be like that of God with us; that is, far beyond the bounds of reason. And we should be like this, because this is how God loves us.

Because it is based purely on religion and springs from the spirit of obedience and devotion to the rule of God, Christ's explanation of the meaning and nature of marriage is also completely super-rational. Whatever men may make of it, God intended marriage to be the mystery of physical and spiritual union, as much for the education of the human race as for its continuation. To think that it is permissible to break off in the middle, when marriage becomes difficult, is to fall short of God's stipulation: "It was not so at the beginning of things" (Matt. 19:8). When men do fail in this respect, others should not, however, judge them, for God alone can judge. Our Lord himself left the woman taken in adultery to God's judgment – in fact it would seem from the context that she was only betrothed, not married, since she was to be stoned, the punishment for infidelity during betrothal, whereas according to the law a married woman would have been strangled. If Christ would not condemn her, how can ordinary men presume to do so? For individuals vary so greatly in their requirements and their abilities. The sanctity of the perfect marriage is attained by few; God knows that many will err and his mercy extends to all. The provisions of civil law which strive to be fair to the conditions of a variety of persons, have nothing to do with the individual's conscience and responsibility before God. Civil law regulates the life of society, according to the expediency of the world; it does not dispense anyone from the dictates of his conscience before God; and everyone has to account to God alone in everything that he does or leaves undone.

Friendship occupies a position of great value in human life and one of the most wonderful things in Jesus' life is the fact that he too experienced friendship. John, Mary Magdalen, Lazarus and his sisters are among his friends and he liked to rest and relax in the house of the last-named. As natural, unembarrassed and unconcerned about etiquette as when he spoke with the Samaritan woman, he greets Magdalen, still overwhelmed by the shock of Good Friday, and calls her by the familiar name, Mary; it is at this that she recognizes him (John 20:16). All this reveals to us the humanity of one who enjoys the freedom given by a true service of God.

2. The ordering of material goods in the light of God's rule can be illuminated by a few fundamental

183

considerations. Since the dignity of man is based on his relationship with God, the difference from the ordinary scale of values is immediately evident. It is not what a man has, but what he is, that makes up his value and dignity. In St. James' epistle this is summed up in the words "Is one of the brethren in humble circumstances? Let him be proud of it; it exalts him, whereas the rich man takes pride in what in truth abases him" (Jas. 1:9, 10). No one, if he is honest, can pride himself on the greatness of his possessions, and no one need feel ashamed because he has less.

As regards commerce in material goods scholastic ethics distinguish between commutative justice, which individuals in business life should practise among themselves, and distributive justice, which assures the individual the share due to him of the goods of the community. As regards the exchange value in private business, individuals may agree among themselves, but on the share of the individual in the common good only the representative of society, the authority of Crown or State, can come to a decision.

Commutative justice will be judged by the religious man, by the man conscious of the kingdom of God, otherwise than by the standards of pure reason. Rational justice would say: "As you do to me, so I'll do to you", but the higher justice of the kingdom of God says: "I can and should waive my rights out of love." I can and should "turn the other cheek" and not "grudge him my coat" too, in order to avoid going to law with my neighbour. On the other hand, where there is responsibility for a communal group, for example in the case of the father of a family, it is necessary to stand up for justice in the face of injustice, because the members of the body are there to help one another and "to make the best advantage" of their talents in the service of others (1 Cor. 12:17). There is, however, no such thing as a schematic regulation of ownership in the name of the kingdom of God: "You have the poor among you always" (Matt. 26:11). There is a natural distinction between rich and poor, just as there is between the efficient and the lazy or, more profoundly, between realists and idealists, introverts and extroverts. But the distinction is a psychological one and tells us nothing about morality or religion. Thus it is of no religious importance whatever whether a man has material possessions or not – the only important point is *how* he has them and how he disposes of them. So in the parable of the pounds given to the ten servants (Luke 19) Jesus does not speak in derogatory terms of the realities of economics: the man who makes ten pounds from his one and the man who similarly makes five from his one are not therefore sinners; on the contrary, they receive their master's thanks, for "he who is trustworthy over a little sum is trustworthy over a greater" (Luke 16:10) and "if a man is rich, gifts will be made to him" (Matt. 13:12). Through their good management they gain even more.

But possessions bring with them their own danger: they threaten the inner freedom and honesty of the "steward", who has nothing which is truly his own personal property and therefore cannot attach himself whole-heartedly to these exterior material goods without doing

185

harm to his soul. The rich young man, who had kept all the commandments since his youth (Luke 18:22f.), had overlooked, according to one of our Lord's apocryphal sayings, that "many of your brothers are dying of hunger and yet your house is full of many delicacies". Everybody knows Christ's severe admonition: "It is easier for a camel to pass through a needle's eye than for a man to enter the kingdom of God when he is rich" (Mark 10:25). But it is necessary to note firstly that the variant of "kingdom of heaven" (Matt. 19:23) into which the rich man enters with difficulty usually means the same as "the kingdom of God", that is God's rule; in other words, the passage means that it is difficult for the rich man to subject himself to the divine rule. Jesus often emphasizes that the refusal of God's call has consequences for a man's eternal life (e.g. John 3:18). Secondly we must note the addition: "What is impossible to man's powers is possible to God" (Luke 18:27). It is not only conceivable but borne out by Christ's own experience, that men who have grace in their souls are able to achieve, in the midst of worldly possessions, that inner freedom which is bestowed on the man living under the rule of God. Abraham "the father of faith", had power over great possessions; the father of the prodigal son, so lovingly characterized, is evidently a rich man; and Jesus had wealthy friends, at least it is suggested that both Lazarus and Nicodemus were such. But these are exceptions to the type: the rich farmer who forgets God in the security of his well-filled barns, the rich man outside whose house Lazarus starved to death. For this reason it pleases the Lord to challenge the typical material-

ism of the age (a materialism which existed then as now):
he does not hesitate to destroy a herd of swine, to convince
one who is possessed that the evil spirit has departed from
him (Matt. 8:28f.). In this way he stresses that the importance of spiritual values is far above that of material ones.

One condition is bound up with ownership and good
management as far as the kingdom of God is concerned:
if you already have valuable material possessions, which
the wise man can only regard as "base wealth" (Knox) –
the old translation "mammon of iniquity" is less apt in
the context – then you should use it "to win yourselves
friends", as the steward did, who was "commended" by
his master for his prudence (Luke 16:8). How could the
master praise him when he had apparently acted with
intent to deceive? The solution of the problem is simple.
There is no question of a deception. The steward, who
was probably dismissed by his master, a big landowner
because of his negligence, conferred with his tenants who
were bound to deliver to him each year the due percentage
of their yield: one a hundred firkins of oil, the other a
hundred quarters of wheat, and so on. Of this, half or
nearly two-thirds went to the owner himself and the
remaining half or third to the steward – quite rightly
since he too had to live. But the steward waives his claim
to the share due to him for this last year of his stewardship:
"Quick, sit down and write it as fifty", he says to the
first tenant. "Here is thy bill, write it as eighty", he says
to the second. In this way the steward makes friends of
the farmers; morally they owe him a debt of gratitude
and when he is in difficulties, they will feel bound to

187

help him. This prudent anticipation of generous abstention is held up to us by Jesus as an example of how we too should look ahead. Anyone who considers his life and his responsibilities in the sight of God, cannot live just for the present; he must not squander his possessions and his income in reckless egoism. He knows that if he preserves his inner freedom in the face of all the temptations of money and uses what he can spare to relieve the distress of a "neighbour" who has perhaps "fallen among thieves", or to remedy the difficulties of a family, or to give pleasure to his friends (how often it was that Jesus himself accepted invitations to eat with his friends!) – all such actions bring their own reward. God's magnanimity cannot be exceeded. Only have faith beyond the bounds of expediency or reason and you will experience it. "Make it your first care to find the kingdom of God, and his approval, and all these things shall be yours without the asking" (Matt. 6:33).

The payment for work accomplished belongs to the sphere of distributive justice. It cannot be calculated schematically and we must take as our ruling that of the kingdom of God: "Do to other men all that you would have them do to you" (Matt. 7:12). St. Francis of Sales explains this in the following way: If you are a businessman, then you as the seller should put yourself into the position of the buyer – and the buyer should put himself in the position of the seller. "You are all brethren alike" (Matt. 23:8) and as children of the one Father we must look for a fair settlement. Ruthless exaggeration of self-love constitutes the sin of egoism, and to withhold the payment due for his work from the worker is an egoism which cries out to heaven: "You have kept back the pay of the workmen who reaped your lands, and it is there to cry out against you; the Lord of hosts has listened to their complaint. You have feasted here on earth, you have comforted your hearts with luxuries on this day that dooms you to slaughter. You have condemned and murdered the innocent man, while he offered no resistance" (Jas. 5:4–6).

But how are we to interpret the parable of the labourers in the vineyard (Matt. 20)? For it is surely unjust that those who were hired later should receive the same wages. The "vineyard" is the kingdom of God into which some are invited sooner, some later – and yet all receive the same grace. Applied to circumstances in this world, the conduct of the employer would certainly not be unjust since no one was cheated of the agreed wages, but it would, nonetheless, be arbitrary. As far as God is concerned, it is otherwise, simply because right from the beginning everything that a man can "earn" in God's service is what is bestowed upon him gratuitously. God may give more to one and less to another, but he gives to all purely out of love and is especially generous to those who in accordance with the truth make no claims but leave all to God. As St. Francis of Sales says: "Demand nothing of God and deny him nothing." To apply this to the human sphere of relationships between employers and employees is, however, meaningless.

To lend money to someone who, in spite of his efforts, is in financial difficulties and not insist on repayment is in accordance with the spirit of brotherhood demanded by

Jesus: "Do to other men . . .". But this does not mean that a capitalist economy with its dividends would contradict Christ's idea of the kingdom of God. It is revealing that the steward who had one pound, in the parable related by Luke, and did not increase it, was blamed because he had not put the money "into the bank, so that I might have recovered it with interest when I came" (Luke 19:23). We see from this that Jesus was attacking only a merciless application of legal right: "The greatest right can become the greatest injustice" was a Roman saying. Charity must not suffer because of "justice".

In the gospels labour is definitely not valued as a cultural asset to the same extent as it is today in Europe and North America. This would be to misunderstand the more easy-going outlook of the Oriental – in so far as the Bible reflects the attitude of the country where it originated. The "conversion" demanded by the kingdom of God is certainly not to be taken as a kind of model five-year plan according to the formulae of modern dictatorships. Labour in the gospels is for the purpose of earning man's daily bread honestly, in the sense in which we ask for it in the Lord's Prayer. Neither the average Oriental nor the disciple of the kingdom of God worries about the future, but the same action does not always have the same cause. The saintly unconcern expressed by the Sermon on the Mount ("See how the birds of the air never sow, or reap, or gather grain into barns . . . . See how the wild lilies grow; they do not toil or spin. . . . Do not fret, then, over tomorrow; leave tomorrow to fret over its own needs") is as little like the indolence of the lazy man as like the

190

rat-race of an affluent society. But the awareness that man "does not live by bread alone" and that Mary, who had time to listen in peace to God's word, had "chosen the best part", this belongs to the wisdom of the gospel.

Jesus himself has given us an unforgettable example as regards working for our daily bread (and even more as regards working for our family): for the greater part of his life he was "the carpenter's son" and lived, as every rabbi did, from the work of his hands. Just as Paul earned his own living as a tent-maker and only occasionally received charitable gifts from Philippi, so Jesus earned his living for about thirty years as *tekton* and was no less the Son, in whom his Father was well pleased, during that time than he was when he finally devoted himself to the preaching of the good news. While it is possible linguistically to interpret his calling as that of a "carpenter", this is certainly not the only interpretation of the word. On the contrary, everything suggests that the word refers to a building contractor or building worker. In his numerous examples of human planning and construction, Jesus often refers to working in stone but never to woodwork. This is probably not accidental; evidently it was part of his own experience. This may point, too, to the source for the wonderful apocryphal saying, according to which the religious man finds God not simply in his worship with the community but in his work also: "Dig the earth and you will find me, lift the stone and you will find me." For God is present, is the motive power, in everything that a man does in the spirit of love and we can find him "in everything".

191

It naturally cannot be left to the discretion of the private person to determine what, according to distributive justice, should be the individual's share in the benefits of the community; this is the function of the State. And that this authority must be heeded is a principle of Jesus (Matt. 22:21) and is stressed too by Paul (Rom. 13:1 ff.). The man who is obedient to God, puts himself under the jurisdiction of the powers of this world. Even foreign rule, which was the great scandal to Jewish national pride made no difference to this principle. It is true that there was a political enthusiast, a member of the nationalist party, in the ranks of his apostles: Simon the Zealot, but we are clearly meant to understand that he was a former supporter of the "Zionism" of the time. Jesus clearly wanted to have nothing to do with the periodic upheavals caused by so-called "Messiahs"; and the anxiety that the common people would put his mission as "king and messiah" on the same level as their political aims made him take flight on one occasion (John 6:15), and on others forbid his disciples to spread abroad who he was and the miracles he wrought (Mark 7:36; 8:30; Luke 9:21). It is because of such conduct that he met with the revenge of the nationalists: he had to undergo the humiliation of seeing Barabbas, a political ringleader, preferred to him and of being crucified between two thieves with the mocking superscription: "Jesus of Nazareth, King (Messiah) of the Jews" (John 19:19).

His approval of State taxation, "Render to Caesar the things that are Caesar's", moreover, suggests that there is room in the kingdom of God for the most varied forms of political expediency that are conceivable. As Jesus himself pays the temple dues for the sake of public order (Matt. 17:23ff.), so the empirical civil power bears "the sword" as the symbol of its authority. There is, moreover, no reference to any fundamental objection being raised by the Lord to military service for the protection of the State (and for the suppression of more or less rebellious provinces) in any of the gospels, in spite of Roman imperialism and the hated "collaboration" of the Herods. It is not expected either of the centurion at Capharnaum, whose professional pride is clearly indicated (Matt. 8:9), or of the converted centurion Cornelius (Acts 10:24ff.), that they should renounce their careers in the name of the kingdom of God. If later on, because of their zeal against the idolatrous worship of the state's omnipotence, Christians found themselves persecuted, it was sometimes out of moral necessity but sometimes too out of ill-advised defiance. It would, however, be historically incorrect and unfair to think of early Christianity up to the time of Constantine as being in a state of constant passive opposition to the State. Persecution was not at all their normal condition; the Roman empire was on principle tolerant towards every religious cult. The anti-semitic measures of Claudius in 49 A.D. (Acts 18:2) and the cruel whims of Nero, Domitian, Trajan, Decius und Diocletian from the first to the third centuries are in complete contrast to the tolerance and even friendliness of more humane emperors. Hadrian, Marcus Aurelius, Alexander Severus and others rescinded the hostile acts of their predecessors, and they also gave positive proof of their own good will in their decrees. The last-named, for instance, legalized the building of Christian churches well before the time of Constantine. When Jesus referred to what was due to Caesar and what was due to God, he did not, of course, imply any fundamental distinction between Church and State, either in the sense of a separation or of a connection of powers. We are entitled, without injury to the kingdom of God, to prefer one or the other of these forms. Considered retrospectively, it is, to say the least, questionable whether Constantine's purely political idea of a State Church was a blessing for Christianity. With Father John Courtney Murray S. J. we may hold the American pattern of the separation of Church and State, in the sense of each being free and independent in its sphere, to be just as valid as the union of the two powers or the medieval idea of the "two swords" in the service of the *sacrum imperium*.

Did the early Christians, perhaps, under the still vivid influence of Jesus' preaching of the kingdom of God, nourish a communistic dream? From a purely religious point of view, any economic order which contributed to the general good, that is, the moral unity of the people, would have been possible in theory; but that the primitive community had any notion at all of inventing its own State-Church economic system, could only be entertained by an over-fertile imagination. Apart from the traditional right to personal property, the Judaeo-Christian ideal, as Luke describes it in the Acts (2:42ff.), was to live according to a brotherhood inspired by religion. They knew that Jesus had required voluntary poverty of his inner

194

circle of disciples and had a common purse instituted, without disputing a man's right to property. The traditional phrase, the "mammon of iniquity", cannot be quoted as opposite evidence, since as we have already observed the actual translation is doubtful. We could, however, describe the life of the early Christians in Jerusalem as a kind of communism of love, if we interpret the words, "All the faithful held together, and shared all they had", in the widest sense according to the context. They were animated by a brotherly community spirit which showed itself in the religious willingness to help all those in need. It is clear that the majority of them were poor, even if the description "the saints of Jerusalem who are in need" is rather an indication of the special reverence to which the community in Jerusalem was entitled as the mother Church of Christianity, and because of its charity towards the Judaeo-Christian community, than a statement of economic fact. Nowhere is there any suggestion of the giving-up of possessions on principle in favour of communal ownership, but solely of the complete willingness and readiness of those with possessions to support their poor brethren.

3. The rule of God in the relationship of time and eternity. If life itself is not the greatest of earthly goods, then other earthly values are even less important. Nonetheless, these values are given to us by God. Frequently in the history of Christianity it has happened that a strong religious awareness of and attachment to the one necessity has given rise to an attitude which tended to disparage earthly values. This was a particular danger at times when the idea of the

kingdom of God was to some extent misunderstood and an erroneously over-literal interpretation led to concentration on the kingdom of heaven, removing the emphasis from the earthly scene to that of the next world. But what Jesus proclaimed was the kingdom of God, the rule of God here and for our present life. The man who "enters into the kingdom of heaven" in Christ's sense, is the man who puts himself at the disposal of the kingdom of God. Such a man possesses eternal life here and now and blessedness in the world to come will be given him into the bargain: the latter is the fruit of his life of faith. The reference to "a rich reward" in heaven (Matt. 5:12) is intended in the same sense; not as something that happens from the outside, but as something that matures inwardly. And the actual idea of a reward is only a secondary motive in a sermon addressed to ordinary people, for the fundamental principle is stated later: "Make it your first care to find the kingdom of God and his approval" – everything else belongs to the things which "shall be yours without the asking", the earthly joys and values as well as the eternal reward.

Heaven, the promised blessedness, is, therefore, not the motive for a man's act of faith; rather it is the reverence he feels towards God who calls him, the love he offers him "with his whole heart, his whole soul, and all his strength". When there is a place for such love in his heart, the call of the good news has attained its goal and God's goodness will bestow everything else, just as he bestows grace itself. It is part of God's grace that he calls men to him and it is "grace answering to grace" when a man receives

Christ's message of salvation and follows his call. It needs "force" to enter the kingdom of heaven (Matt. 11:12) and even father and mother must be set aside (Luke 14:26) if human attachments stand in the way. "Hating his father and mother" should not be interpreted literally; what is meant and what is implied by the meaning of the word in the everyday language of the Jews is "to value less, to set aside" in favour of greater things. The greater thing is God, who is greater than everything.

"In anxious fear", says Paul, "you must work to earn your salvation" (Phil. 2:12). This admonition too needs the explanation provided by an understanding of the contemporary language of Jewish tradition. It is in anxious fear – "he dared not look on the open sight of God" – that Moses loosens his shoes from his feet when he trembles in God's presence. Fear and amazement are experienced by Peter at the miraculous draught of fishes: "Leave me to myself, Lord; I am a sinner." All these feelings are of an intense mystical emotion at the sign of God's nearness. Similar language is used in the evangelist's accounts describing the people when they witnessed the signs worked by Jesus: "they praised God, full of awe", that is, they were "filled with amazement" at something they could not understand and could only praise the miraculous power of God. And the same emotion is experienced by the believer, says St. Paul, when he sees the incomprehensible condescension of divine love which is manifested in Christ. This is what the words "in anxious fear" mean in their context: deeply moved by the glory of God's grace, which is deserved by no one, we

197

should concern ourselves seriously with our salvation in that spirit of selfless devotion, for which Christ himself is our model.

Does not Jesus' proclamation of the kingdom of God awaken an undertone of fear or anxiety as well? He proclaims, after all, the judgment of all those who close their minds to his message. He will say to them: "Go far from me, you that are accursed into that everlasting fire" (Matt. 25:41). It cannot be denied that the images of hell – even when we remember that they were not invented by Christ, but were a part of Jewish tradition, which contains in its religious history analogous and even more terrifying pictures of hell – are intended to frighten. They are addressed to the man who remains unmoved by any other appeals. For there exists a spiritual apathy which is only shattered, if at all, by fear. Whether afterwards anything more is brought into play, whether deeper layers of religious feeling are aroused, is another and wider question upon which depends the seriousness of the religious conversion. Education may well start with the "fear of slaves" provided it does not stop there, and Christ's certainly does not stop there. He speaks in images of the dreadfulness of the fate of those who harden their hearts against God's call; but those who follow it are set free from fear. They are encouraged by Jesus to call God their "Father" and children do not fear their father, but place their trust in him. As far as the images of the next world are concerned, their meaning is explained by John: "For the man who believes in him there is no rejection; the man who does not believe is already rejected" (John 3:18): he judges himself, he remains without and will not enter into the kingdom, into the knowledge of those things "which God has prepared for them who love him".

In Hofmannsthal's lyrical drama *Das kleine Welttheater* (The Little Theatre of the World) the reality of this other-worldly dimension is suggested to the spectator: the man who refused the call when on earth is left standing at the door of the heavenly communion of the blessed, as though spell-bound; while the others go in he cannot enter. We can find analogies here on earth. Perhaps Dante's pictures of the poet's journey through hell, purgatory and heaven are meant as images of man's spiritual life on earth. And many of us have gone through times when it seemed to us that we had fallen prey to the devil and were without faith or hope. Saints, too, like Jane Frances Chantal or Theresa of Lisieux, suffered hours, even weeks and months of darkness, abandonment and unbelief – in the rational and emotional levels of the soul, if not in the very depths of the mental self where the yearning for God persists. At such times we should keep in mind the unfathomable mystery of Christ's own feeling of abandonment when he hung on the cross. For he prays in the words of the twenty-first psalm, which begins: "My God, my God, why hast thou forsaken me?" In his dire need he takes as his prayer the messianic sacrificial liturgy; "it is fitting that the Head should speak at the same time for the members", Augustine says in explanation of this passage. Yet it was also his own distress, suffered in common with many of his "God-forsaken" brethren, and

199

his own moving prayer offered for those who in their bitterness "know not what they do"; it was a brother's plea that God should not heed their bitter words but only his prayer, for "it was not as if our high priest were incapable of feeling for us in our humiliations; he has been through every trial, fashioned as we are, only sinless" (Heb. 4:15). Through him and because of him "we can appear boldly before God", trusting in his eternal love, "and he will grant all our requests" (1 John 3:22), since his love is far greater than anything we know or could conceive.

God's message to us is one of tremendous simplicity. Only one thing is necessary, the sincere consecration of a man's heart to God who calls him. Everything else in the religious sphere is on the level of penultimate importance, mediating, helping towards this first requirement. It matters only in so far as it serves the rule of God. The old laws were reduced by Jesus, the lawgiver, to their essentials and the traditions of his forefathers measured against the one thing that is necessary. The fuller measure of the justice (piety) which he preached (Matt. 5:20) is not based on a greater number of laws nor on a greater strictness in their fulfilment, but on the pure surrender of the heart to the Father in heaven. Only this one thing is necessary and in this is perfection. "For my yoke is easy, and my burden light" (Matt. 11:30). Even the mediator himself, Jesus Christ, through whom God's call comes to man in human form and human signs, tells us of himself only that he comes from the Father to lead to the Father all who trust in him; that he intercedes for us with the Father to save us from the power of evil and to make us the people of God, the communion of the sanctified; and that he does all this through his spirit, the spirit of love. For himself he desires nothing but what his name tells us: to be the saviour of his brethren, to lead them into the kingdom in which God's loving will is taken up and carried out by men. And because this was his sole desire, which he proved by his death, God has glorified him and given him the name above all names: "the holy one", the prototype of holiness; "the high priest" and "intercessor"; "the origin and the crown of all faith" (Heb. 12:2); " the mediator and saviour", the redeemer.

It is, therefore, not of decisive importance whether a man has a more or less perfect theological knowledge of Christ's mystery and a more or less pure concept of God, whether the traditions among which he lives are Judaic or Hellenic, highly civilized or primitive. What matters is that he should hear God's call, whatever the form in which it comes to him. He will find evidence of it in the splendours of creation and the judgments of world history, in his heart's own longing and his conscience's admonitions, in the prophets and ultimately in God's Son, the revelation of his goodness and kindness to man. Even he speaks of the mystery of God only in images and through his own life, which tells us more than any words could. Our human idea of God is limited even in God's revelation. We have only approximate images of God and the degree to which they are like him is always balanced by an equal degree of unlikeness. "Who can say what God is like?" St. Augustine asked. "I dare to claim, brethren, that perhaps John too did not tell of what he is like, but spoke as he did because he was speaking as a man about God. We talk of 'three Persons', not because in doing so we could do justice to the reality, but in order not to remain wholly silent. . . . The qualities we attribute to God, concepts like 'righteous' and so on, do not equal his sublimity, which is beyond all human conception. And yet Scripture is right to use these words: for through any and all possible words the spirit shall be led gradually to that which cannot be comprehended in words." But the nearest possible idea of God is given in the life and words of him who came from heaven: "the only-begotten Son, who abides in the bosom of the Father" (John 1:18). We must put all our trust in the Father who loves us "with unchanging love" (Jer. 31:3), for he is "a Lord none ever trusted in vain" (Isa. 49:23) and "everything helps to secure the good of those who love God" (Rom. 8:28).

What the joyful message of Jesus teaches us beyond this is the breadth of the spirit and its ability to recognize the signs of divine intervention in human history. The message of the kingdom of God does not justify a spiritual narrow-mindedness on the part of those who feel themselves the heirs of Abraham. There are many religions, that is, many concepts of the ineffably great mystery in and above man, and many different human civilizations. It was not Christ's wish to add another religion to the many, but rather to reduce them all to their real meaning, beginning with the religion of Israel since, according to Christ himself, "salvation, after all, is to come from the Jews" (John 4:22). But salvation does not depend on Israel; "the spirit bloweth, where it listeth" and the light shines everywhere in human darkness. "The man who is not against you is on your side", Christ said (Mark 9:40), and no one is against him who seeks the kingdom of God in so far as he can. Jesus often chooses examples of true religious dedication from among the Samaritans, regarded by the Jews as heretics, in order to shame the proud. "From east and west", from all nations and cultures, he sees the children of the kingdom entering – but those Pharisees who thought "they had won acceptance with God and despised the rest of the world", did not go home "in God's favour".

But this does not imply that the different forms of religion in the world are equal in relevance or value. Jesus himself loved and prized the religion of the chosen people above all others; so much so that he only amended it in certain all-too-human interpretations, while retaining and using its spirit of divine worship, as it is expressed in the traditional prayers of Israel, as the basis for the divine praise of the New Covenant, culminating in his commemorative feast. He came as the fulfilment of the religious searching of all mankind. He is "the way, the truth and the life". Incorporation in his mystical body, membership of the kingdom of God, cannot be measured purely according to exterior demarcations, even though his faithful form a New Covenant, a community or church with definite conditions of membership, which those outside can see and accept. What cannot be seen by men is the essence of religious life, the individual's self-dedication to God's call.

When the joyful tidings were announced by the angels

they sang: "Glory to God in high heaven and peace on earth to men that are God's friends" (Luke 2:14); that is, to the men called by the love and grace of God, who is sublime above all human conception.

The Image of Mary

ONE of the most attractive aspects of Christian piety is the love and respect which Christ's followers show and always have shown for his mother. Human and religious emotions intermingle when we contemplate her life as a mother, her spiritual development to maturity from her first intimacy with the child through the stages of withdrawal and self-effacement as she recognizes the autonomy of his mission: we see her first shock at the behaviour of the twelve-year old (Luke 2:48–50), the stress on *his* hour at Cana (John 2:4), on *his* vocation when she and his relatives come to speak with him (Mark 3:31 ff.). These proofs of her love as a mother have their fruit in the profound union between Son and mother, which can be seen at his final sacrifice (John 19:25). Such a life is not only moving in its human relevance as a model for all mothers, but has a religious significance too, as the image of man's attainment of grace and sanctification through complete surrender of the heart, through entering into and submitting to "the kingdom of God", as Jesus called it. These humanly and spiritually moving facts are presented by the evangelists in the brief outlines of an objective narrative, which cannot possibly have been intended propaganda for a cult. Such a cult would have been as inconceivable in the Jewish world as among the Greek mystery religions, with their cults of Astarte and Isis; and certainly suspect for the disciples of the kingdom of God.

It is, however, revealing for an elucidation of the spiritual relationship between the first disciples and the mother of Jesus that Paul's travelling companion Luke, who was close to him in his radical Christ-centredness, dwelt with the greatest of loving care on the recollections of Christ's youth and Mary's experiences as a mother. A happy dispensation of Providence sent him on the track of the record written in Aramaic, which (according to a well-founded hypothesis of modern exegetes) had been transcribed by a priest known to Elizabeth, Mary's cousin and friend, and which so preserved in literary form Mary's intimate accounts of Jesus' conception, birth and early youth.[1] Among these reminiscences, which were written down long before the spread of the Christian mission, we have the *Magnificat,* Mary's prophecy inspired by the Holy Spirit of how all future generations would call the mother of Christ blessed (Luke 1:48).

As far as the first disciples were concerned, it was as a matter of course that they ascribed to Christ's mother a personal share in the development of her son's spiritual life, since they themselves had first of all learned to know and

[1] See P. Gaechter, *Maria im Erdenleben* (1953), pp. 62ff.

love the man Christ and only gradually had recognized the supernatural in him. The mother, after all, is the first and most real character-forming influence in the early and decisive years of a child's life. We must try to imagine what it means that God entered into our human nature, became a man like us in everything but without sin (Heb. 4:15), and grew up, advancing "in wisdom with the years, and in favour both with God and men" (Luke 2:52). The Jewish writer Shalom Asch, drawing on his deep knowledge of and insight into the Jewish customs of that time, describes vividly in his book on Mary how the parents would have told their child marvellous stories of the patriarchs and instructed him in the main points of the law, the faithfulness of God and the faithlessness of the people, and the longing for the promised kingdom of the future. His mother would have taught him the first prayers, which were part of the day for every Jewish family: the sublime praises of Jehovah for the gifts of nature, for the delivery of his people out of slavery into the promised land, and supplications that his name might be held sacred and that they might always be ready to do his will. We cannot doubt that the fundamental religious disposition of the child's spiritual life flowered as much because of the human help he received, as because of his innate intimacy with the Father in heaven. We find confirmation of this in the form of his prayer, new and yet not so new, the Our Father. Paul calls his pupil Timothy happy in that his mother and grandmother, Eunice and Lois, handed on to him the faith and piety which now animates him (2 Tim. 1:5); and most of us would acknowledge the same of our own experience and give sincere thanks for it. It is thus not a rash observation on Paul's part when he attributes to Christ at his first moment of human consciousness the words, "I am coming . . . to do thy will, O my God" (Heb. 10:7). In their humility these words echo those spoken by Mary his mother when she conceived him. She kept all these things in her heart and lived her life according to them. Sometimes she was surprised, even afraid, when he said, for instance: "Could you not tell that I must needs be in the place which belongs to my Father?" or "Nay, woman, why dost thou trouble me with that? My time has not come yet" or "If anyone does the will of God, he is my brother, and sister and mother", but she reflected on all these things and kept them in her heart until the final fulfilment.

She lived on after this for a time in the circle of the apostles, quietness hiding her greatness and humility disguising her blessedness, and witnessed their early preaching of Jesus, as Messiah and Lord. She died early on; that it was early we can now deduce with some probability if not with complete certainty from the sources: from the archaic form of the account, the style of the narrative still reminiscent of the Old Testament, which would have undergone at least some adaptation to the language of early Christian preaching if it had been communicated by word of mouth to the evangelists. But it was regarded as more fitting to leave the documentary heritage of a deceased person unaltered. Her legacy and her memory remained dear to the apostles. All of them felt that Christ's words to John, whom he loved especially, were addressed to them too. John relates with gratitude how the dying Lord committed his mother to his care: "This is thy mother." So it remains today: she is our mother by virtue of the fact that she was chosen to bear in her womb the first-born of the new mankind, and so also mankind itself, and by virtue of her perfection in grace which unites her with him who is our brother for ever.

This wonderful inspired picture of God's elective love comes truly to life in the unobtrusive phrases of reverence and love, which we read in the gospels. Looking at a picture by one of the old masters, or listening to a Mozart sonata which has inspired and influenced many generations, we may trace individual features, touches, colours, as elements of a beautiful whole, try to interpret the artist's intentions in these details. We may hold forth with a critic's ingenious arguments on the masterpiece as a whole or its details. But either we understand the whole work as a gift of grace or we rationalize about it and destroy the mystery with conceptual subtleties. It is the picture as a whole which matters. So, it seems to us, we can trace God's love for man in the picture of Mary, mother and handmaid, as the evangelists have drawn it, and all the details will be meaningful as elements of the whole. Yet the picture is of importance for Christian life more when it is appreciated from the heart than when it is the subject of abstract analysis or dialectic. Theology is to real religious experience, what natural science is to life itself or art-criticism is to real art. All the details discovered by theologians, the "art-critics" of the biblical picture, attest the zeal of connoisseurs who vie with one another in their findings. God's creation is a whole, and we must comprehend the picture which we contemplate as a whole. And any greater degree of understanding which is achieved will have been attained by the experience and the imitation of that reverent love which guided the "painter" of the picture of Mary in the gospel. It was the "artist's intention" to give praise to the blessed mother in her whole being, to the glory of God in her grace. Inspired by the divine Spirit the "artist" is telling us that Mary was the handmaid of the mystery of God's generous love and was therefore called blessed, and it was in this attitude that she was found worthy of reverence by the disciples of Christ.

For us a created being cannot be the object of worship, as such – or at least only in a very vague, derivative sense, in so far as we may revere a human person and commend ourselves to his goodwill, without actually praying to him. Theology distinguishes between the worship of God and the veneration of the saints. As far as prayer and the religious cult are concerned, Bernard Häring[2] says: With the saints "dialogue" is possible, but by comparison with our worship of God, it can only be termed so "in an analogical sense". As the meaning of this sentence seemed unclear to me, I asked the author what the phrase "only in an analogical sense" meant with reference to the worship of God. He replied that whereas "dialogue" can be used of God and of the saints in the same sense, "prayer" cannot be used in the same but only in an analogical sense. Here he is clearly in agreement with Newman who ex-

[2] *The Law of Christ* II (1961), p. 534, note 170.

210

plained that we can ask the blessed for their intercession and we can venerate them, but not more. Worship, adoration in the deepest sense of faith and cult, trust in grace, redemption and salvation, can only be rendered to God. In other words, we pray to the saints similarly yet fundamentally differently from how we pray to God. Thus the Church prays to God the Father "through Christ in the unity of the Holy Spirit" and *communicantes,* that is, in spiritual association with the best of our brothers and sisters and especially with "glorious Mary ever a virgin, mother of God and of our Lord Jesus Christ". The Church commends to us the direct invocation of the saints, without stressing it in her official prayers. She leaves it to the needs of piety; and those who would be content with liturgical practice alone should in no sense be blamed, provided that they do not reject direct dialogue with the saints, since this is after all "prayer in an analogical sense".

Veneration of Mary has in the course of centuries developed beyond early Christian practice in two respects. In the first place as regards theological statements about her treasury of grace which can be discovered in the biblical account of her; and secondly as regards the manner in which her veneration is expressed in popular devotion. Basically some development is natural in every religion, because it is experienced through history by changing generations and nations in different stages of civilization. As far as the theological unfolding of the Christian Revelation is concerned, a conceptual development of the mystery of Jesus Christ can already be recognized in the apostles' preaching of the Word. In order to communicate their convictions to others the apostles had to put into human words and to elucidate according to their understanding their faith in Christ as the personal union of the divine and the human; in this task they were strengthened by the promise of the Holy Spirit. The declarations of the early Councils, too, formulated against the Arians, were explanations of Christian doctrine necessitated by the time and are accepted by all Christians although they go beyond the biblical statements, the significance of which was after all controversial. There is a similar development in the case of Marian theology and popular devotion, in which can be clearly seen the interaction of the teaching office of the Church and popular sentiment: the definition of Mary as Mother of God at the Council of Ephesus in 431 – the very place where once had flourished the cult of Artemis-Astarte (Acts 19:23 ff.) – was actually brought about largely by popular opinion. But who could, on that account, see in the veneration of the mother of Christ the continuation of the pagan mother-cult? It was the same with regard to the individual features of Mary's excellence, which loving veneration derives from the biblical picture of her. They are due to the Mother of Christ, not to the object of a religious cult for its own sake; they are relevant to the election of Mary to Christ's service and mission; they are intended for the most blessed member of the body of Christ, who is for that reason the prototype of all the blessed. We see all this vividly in the liturgy of the Church. For the Church's prayer is naturally theocentric, continuing in the spirit of the Old Testament and yet distinguished from the Jewish liturgy through the addition of "in the name of Jesus" and "through Christ our Lord", the mediator of the New Covenant. Just as, however, the saints of the Old Law were held to be intercessors for the earthly members of the people (as is indicated by the appearance of Moses and Elias at the Transfiguration of the Lord), so God's people of the New Testament know that on earth they are yet one with the choirs of the heavenly Sion, the blessed apostles, the martyrs, and above all the holy mother of Christ, whom all generations call blessed, and they all share in the rejoicing of that heavenly Jerusalem (Heb. 11:22 ff.).

It is through the idea and the ground of mariology – the reverent commemoration of the blessed mother of Christ – that its very measure and proportion are derived. Veneration of Mary is part of the veneration of Christ and from this draws its meaning, proportion and limits. What matters alone is the rule of God through Christ's grace. But the idea is inevitably only imperfectly realized by us on earth. Certain historical aberrations in the Church's development are not a proof that the Church has fallen away from her mission, but that she is made up of imperfect human beings, who need constantly to reflect upon and measure themselves against the idea, which is there for us to read in the apostolic sources. The basic principles of this duty of reflection in the face of aberrations or confusions have been emphasized repeatedly by eminent theologians and spiritual writers. The promise of the Holy Spirit is that the content of Revelation will be preserved by God's grace, in spite of the shortcomings of the human element in the Church which constitute a constant threat. It is common knowledge that such eclipses and defects in Christian life were profound and even lasted for generations: for example, the temporal claims of the Church in the Middle Ages compared with the actual concept of the kingdom of God; the neglect of the Mass as the communal celebration of the faithful and of the Bible as the true manual of theology and primer for the people; the asceticism of the doctrine of perfection carried to a hatred of the body and nature under neo-Platonic and Manichean influences; "westernization" in the missions, that is, a lack of willingness to adapt to Christianity the different ways of thought of different peoples, as was done in the apostolic era with cultures as different as the Jewish and Greek. All these examples are merely indications which should explain why on the plane of piety too and in the different emphases of different ages in theological matters, perfection on earth is not to be expected.

Devotion to Mary in the West, in spite of its importance as part of the Christian whole, has at times since the Middle Ages, due perhaps to the courtly cult of woman, degenerated into the sentimental or erotic. In this it differs considerably from the image of the Madonna venerated in the East. Protests came from the greatest churchmen. St. Bernard, a very devoted servant of Mary, attacked the contemporary excesses, especially questionable visionary experiences; the Council of Trent castigated popular abuses;[3] and many intellectual and spiritually eminent men,

---

[3] Cf. J. Leclercq, *Grandeur et misère de la dévotion mariale au Moyen Âge* (Maison-Dieu 1954).

such as Peter Canisius, Petavius, Gerson, Benedict XIV and Cardinal Newman made to some extent sharp criticism of certain aspects of the devotion, not to mention the frank and engaging though critical comments of St. Theresa of Lisieux on current sermons on our Lady. Pastors and theologians in our day have referred to obvious weaknesses in biblical and christological education and see the causes in an over-emphasis of Marian aspects. In view of certain excessive expressions of popular emotion bishops have warned the faithful in their Marian devotion not to depart from the spirit of the Bible and of the tradition of the Church and to maintain prudence and discretion regarding apparitions and sensational data. In Latin countries aberrations are much more numerous than in Northern lands. Recent popes have, it is true, commended devotion to Mary as a particularly simple and sure way to reach a true communion with Christ. Indeed, as children this was our way to the saviour: like the shepherds we found him on his mother's knee. But it is not the intention of the Church to nourish incongruities; theologians and pastors ought to preserve due proportions. It has been suggested, not without reason, that far too many theologians provide themselves with a comfortable alibi of Marian essays and writings, and that important theological and pastoral issues are thus neglected. As we said certain exaggerations in the praise of Mary are in many cases concomitant with weaknesses in devotion to Christ himself.

K. Adam and other theologians offer the explanation that since the time when the Church had to defend herself against Arianism, she has set great store in her instruction on giving particular prominence to the divinity of Christ to counter any Arian tendencies. Due to these efforts the humanity of Christ receded imperceptibly into the background. Now according to the epistle to the Hebrews, which is corroborated by the gospels, God became man, became our brother in human nature like us in all characteristics, differing from us only in one: in his proximity to his Father and his perfect devotion to him, that is his sinlessness. In all else he is like us, "born of woman, subject to the law"; like us he learnt from his parents, from the Holy Scripture of the Old Testament, from the natural world and his daily intercourse with people; he worked and prayed, he rejoiced with his friends and suffered in sympathy with the people; he called the people to a reappraisal in accordance with his mission; he had hopes which were shattered by the opposition of the many; he underwent a bitter struggle, a real agony, knowing the persecution and the suffering on the cross which lay before him; but he was obedient and his obedience to his mission was put to the test and found to be faithful even unto death. Now in glory yet still in his humanity, he makes intercession for us in heaven, our great mediator, brother and friend. It is true that the other intercessors, especially his blessed Mother, are not to be separated from him, but they possess only a participation or share in his intercession and he himself is the one great mediator, for "it is not as if our high priest was incapable of feeling for us in our humiliations; he has been through every trial, fashioned as we are" (Heb. 4:15).

Nonetheless, the faithful are far from having a proper

216

awareness of all this, even though it is set out so clearly in the liturgy that indeed it can only be celebrated with full understanding from this point of view. Thus it is essential that it should be constantly and not merely occasionally emphasized. Many of us have experienced, when as children we were prepared for Holy Communion, the alienating awesomeness of the Lord's divine majesty which imposed a distance between him and us and this "empty space" which should have been filled by the humanity of Christ, our brother and mediator, was occupied instead by the merciful, ever-helpful, heavenly Mother. What we are told in the Bible about him, is transferred and reapplied to her, who certainly prays for us too (and all the saints with her) but only in conjunction with him and as secondary intercessors.

We ought certainly to understand the need of preachers and pastors in Latin countries in their presentation to take into account the spiritual disposition of their people. To demand of someone from these countries the same piety expressed in the same emotional and stylistic terms as our own would be as ridiculous as expecting a spiritual writer or preacher of the Baroque age, such as Abraham a Sancta Clara or Martin von Cochem, to express himself in a modern style. Of course, the opposite is equally true: we are in no sense obliged to adopt everything that in the different national churches has been conditioned by personal or popular taste; we must maintain our Christian freedom in the face of the pious subjectivity which is often to be found, especially in matters associated with Mary. "What revolts one's reason" wrote François Mauriac,

217

"are the fabrications at the margin of dogma with which priests embroider their sermons." The Rome correspondent of the *Herder-Korrespondenz* (October 1954) reporting on the Marian Congress, felt compelled to observe that "the profusion of subjects treated is astonishing, even dismaying . . . . The whole gamut was run from the serious statement of problems to subtle sophistries."

Two appellations in particular, which in Holy Scripture are reserved for the Lord, are sometimes used almost as catchwords to excite popular feeling in expectation of the Holy See's declaring new Marian dogmas in response to a "general desire". These are the predicates mediatrix and co-redemptrix. The term "mediatrix of all graces" can be understood correctly when explained theologically, in so far as Mary bore the saviour of the world and makes intercession for the universal intentions of the kingdom of God. But according to Scripture there is surely "only one mediator between God and men, Jesus Christ, who is a man, like them, and gave himself as a ransom for them all" (1 Tim. 2:5f.) and who "lives on still to make intercession on our behalf" (Heb. 7:25). In Northern countries there is certainly a danger of misconceptions in this sphere. Popular awareness of Christ as the one mediator is far from being as alive as it would be, if it corresponded to the preaching of the apostles and to the liturgy. Even greater care ought to be exercised by responsible pastors among uneducated people in Latin and Latin-American countries as far as the impact of such titles on their communities is concerned. It is not easy to avoid giving the impression that between us and him, the one mediator, the majestic

218

judge in anticipation of his final coming, we need the mild and motherly Lady to step forward as our true mediatrix. A priest-friend who worked in Argentina for many years, writing to me shortly before his death, described the "displacement of Jesus Christ" by the cult of Mary in South America: "Here it is Mary who does everything, absolutely everything. God has delegated all power to her and for many Christ exists only in the host. These conditions could in time develop to the stage when the Word of God in Holy Scripture was, even is, practically inaccessible to the people." Unless such appellations are to result in a distortion of the central truth of Christian teaching a great deal of instruction would be necessary in the first place. It would have to emphasize that the risen Lord in his humanity is the first and common intercessor and mediator of all graces and that Mary can, therefore, only act as mediatrix in co-operation with him; that the sacraments are effective by the power of Christ *ex opere operato* and are independent of the intercessions of Mary or any other saints; that in addition to Mary all the saints and all the faithful on earth are in the same sense mediators and intercessors, since we are all enabled and called upon to help one another to salvation through our prayers, our witness, and our love. One might reasonably ask whether in view of the terrible shortage of priests and catechists the time and energy required to explain all this ought not to be devoted instead to expounding the really essential themes of the apostolic message.

Similar objections are valid for the appellation "co-redemptrix". While official quarters have shown reserve, some writers and preachers bandy this catchword about, often among inadequately instructed people. One of the theologians of the Marian Congress already mentioned even believed to have found the key to all Mary's glory in this title. The meaning is rightly explained by theologians in the sense of a "receptive" co-redemption, in so far as Mary, when chosen to be the mother of Christ, gave her assent to the Incarnation and proved her willingness in spiritual union with Christ even to the final sacrifice. Yet we ought not to forget that under the cross beside her stood John and the women of Galilee who were of the same mind. Indeed, all the faithful, in praying the Mass, as generally in the act of faith, are associated with the intention of the saviour, offering "petition, prayer, entreaty . . . for all mankind" that they may attain salvation (1 Tim. 2:1). The liturgy of the Church's year contains occasions rich enough for nourishing and encouraging a fervent devotion to Mary within the framework of the Catholic tradition. We might indeed wonder whether there is nothing left in Holy Scripture or in the sacramental mysteries of the Church to justify having recourse to ever "new" stimulants, not in order to deepen our appreciation of the old truths but to discuss new, hitherto unknown terminological possibilities.

It is significant that in all this private revelations play a psychological rôle which cannot but cause anxiety to those charged with proclaiming the kingdom of God.[4] Here we pass from the realm of theological mariology to

[4] Cf. Karl Rahner, *Visions and Prophecies* (Eng. tr. 1963).

that of popular piety. The host of visionary apparitions in our time is likely to effect religious feeling to the extent that faith depends upon outward chance and not upon the God-centredness of the Bible. The propagation of such apparitions has very little to do with apostolic witness and is not without the danger of promoting religious emotionalism as a substitute for simple and sincere service rendered to the kingdom of God. Psychologically it is easy to understand that, at times of distress and fear, people should be particularly susceptible to all sorts of prophecies of salvation and damnation, to occult phenomena and visible signs of comfort or warning from heaven. But we cannot dismiss the idea that most of these are projections of unconscious longings. Teachers on mysticism agree with psychologists and historians that corporeal visions as such are of a subjective nature.[5] The so-called imaginative apparitions may certainly contain a genuine core, an illumination with corresponding impulses, but their sense elements, forms and voices can be explained as unconscious products of the imagination. St. John of the Cross and Cardinal Newman both recognized this distinction between the divine and human parts of genuine visionary experiences; we need not refer to the innumerable purely subjective experiences which in troubled times shoot up like mushrooms on loosened ground. Someone rightly said of the numerous apparitions of our Lady in our time that it is not Mary who seems to be speaking to us but rather the tortured soul of Western man. There is also

[5] See Aquinas, *Summa Theol.* III, 85, 3 c.

221

a craving for sensation on the part of the masses; the unusual attracts. The stigmata of some devout person have a more powerful effect on the imagination than the Eucharist has on faith. What God revealed once and for all in Jesus Christ is thought to be already known and, without thinking much about it, men search for new "signs from heaven". Jesus always wholly rejected such an attitude. The "demarcation" of the spirits, such as the teachers of the Church evolved with regard to many experiences, seems to many to be no longer required, when innocent children are the recipients of messages from heaven. In fact, it is precisely in these cases that caution is needed to an even greater degree.

All the great mystics agree on the following criteria for private revelations: (1) the matter must contain no questionable element (2) the person concerned should possess maturity of judgment, moral independence and personal holiness – even the mystical state of grace is sometimes stipulated before authenticity may even be considered; (3) as regards the effect there should be evidence of obvious blessings, without detriment to the Christian life of the people. Indeed, only when a positive response can be given to all these criteria can the notion of authentic phenomena be entertained. Of the private revelations submitted to the Roman office in recent years almost all have been judged not to be genuine. The official list of such revelations is far from complete since the majority did not even reach Rome. What is striking regarding the actual matter of these visionary revelations is their spiritual poverty and inadequate content when compared with the message of Christ and his apostles: tears over the state of the world, admonitions to conversion and penance, dreadful threats of what will happen if the "insults to Mary" are not atoned for, demands for a chapel to be built at such or such a place. We are bound to wonder whether the humble handmaid of the Lord would really speak like this.

If the Church's accepted teachers are right in their second criterion to insist on the moral and spiritual maturity of the person receiving the revelation, then we cannot judge the Church's caution in the case of children's visions to be exaggerated. Sometimes there is quoted the cry of hosanna with which the boys who had joined the crowds at Jesus' entry into Jerusalem acclaimed him (Matt. 21:15f.). But this is not proof to the contrary. It has nothing to do with the "visions and private revelations" of children. Children are particularly worthy of love but they do not in the Bible appear as bearers of divine revelations to mankind. We must not confuse the spirit of childlikeness, which the Lord puts before us, with the call to be a witness for the word of God. The Church lays down a minimum age for the holy office; it is obvious that something similar for the "prophets" of the Church is essential. In addition, at the time just before puberty, according to reliable statistics, children are particularly susceptible to visionary experiences and it is a commonplace, noted by psychologists, that this spreads from one child to another.

As far as effects are concerned, actual blessings obtained in the cases of some apparitions approved by the Church

223

are impressive, for instance those at Paray le Monial, Lourdes and Fátima. Even great blessings can, however, only be accepted as proof of the direct divine origin of the vision with reservations and only when the other criteria too are taken into account. Loreto, for example, is a holy place and many holy people bear witness to the blessings they received there, and yet Loreto is not what the pilgrims imagine it to be: the true house of Nazareth. Miraculous answers to prayers are not confirmation of the revelation in question, but are the results of the prayer of faith, which we know to need no particular place to be effective, but which nonetheless gains special strength from the spiritual atmosphere of a holy place. Besides there are non-Christian parallels which are equally remarkable. Pilgrimages to Mecca, to the Ganges, to the holy mountain in Japan have been shown in the spiritual experience of devout pilgrims to be rewarded by great blessings. Who, indeed, could deny or think it impossible that God can show his grace to believers everywhere who hope in salvation, notwithstanding the imperfect religious notions through which they worship the divine mystery?

As an example of enlightened instruction of the faithful in these matters, we might refer to the pastoral letter of Bishop Fléchier of Nîmes in 1706. On a hill near Nîmes a large cross, the work of a great artist, had been erected with the bishop's permission. Soon there were pilgrimages, cures, conversions and visionary revelations of the supposedly miraculous origin of the cross. Many people cut off particles for themselves and the cross was being gradually scraped away. At this point the bishop intervened with his pastoral letter. Concerning the misleading "revelations" he put the matter in the right perspective, explained the miracle-working power of the prayer of faith, warned against a cult of the "material" cross, as though it contained miraculous power, and forbade the attestation of cures by persons other than those officially appointed.[6]

The Church has approved some few private revelations of remote and more recent times but in no case has formally pronounced on their direct divine origin, nor could she do so, according to the official declarations themselves, in a manner binding in faith. The Church's mission is to preserve the general revelation which ended with the apostles, and if need be to examine also the content of private revelations; it is not her task to examine the mental health of the recipient, with the consequent obligation to believe in the direct divine origin of a private revelation as distinct from human influences. Everyone has, therefore, the right, as authoritative statements of Popes Benedict XIV and St. Pius X emphasize, to maintain a cautious or even critical attitude towards revelations (visions or prophecies) even those commended by the Church, and to ascribe or not ascribe to them human faith – to ascribe "divine faith" with complete assent is anyhow excluded. Moreover, the Church emphasizes that the decisive reasons for official commendation are to be found in the matter only, that is to say in the religious object, or in the pilgrimages to holy places. Private revelations are thus to serve at the most as an

---

[6] *Œuvres choisies,* ed. H. Bremond (1911), pp. 107ff.

occasion for recognizing the object which they serve to recommend.

As regards the so-called "miracle of the sun", the "most striking corroboration from heaven" as many people believe, we might remember following points: 1. In many places the same manifestation has been experienced by many people, also in connection with the vision of an impostor as in Gimigliano or of those obviously deceived as at Heroldsbach in Germany or Ghiaia and Aquaviva in Italy. An "earthly" explanation is, therefore, indicated, unless, as at Fátima, the preceding announcement can suggest a supernatural meaning. 2. An earthly explanation of the sun phenomenon is confirmed by experimental observations which everyone can make for himself. While it is dangerous to look into the sun when it is high in the sky, it is possible, according to the experiments of the meteorologist Dr. Stöckl of Regensburg, to gaze into the sun for several minutes when it is not so high in the sky and there is a slight haze in the atmosphere without any harm ensuing; however, due to irritation of the retina the kind of perceptions connected with the "sun-miracle" arise, without there being any need for the heavenly interpretation of the occurrence.

When we consider the effects of numerous visionary experiences, we may ask ourselves whether the undeniable beneficial results are not cancelled out by considerable harm done to the faithful who are being distracted from the message of Christ towards these borderline phenomena of mysticism. It was still relatively harmless when, for instance, in the Basque country after the visions at Fátima a whole crowd of children claimed to have seen the mother of God, since there was no significant message involved. Far worse, as symptoms of the general spiritual outlook, were the events at Heroldsbach – and not only there. In view of the well-known number of such visions in our times and the response they awaken among simple people, it is only too understandable that many people are concerned about the danger of the Christian faith being side-tracked from proclaiming, as Jesus did, the kingdom of God. The essence of the Christian message as proclaimed by the apostles is communion with God through Christ and practical love of our neighbour expressed in corporal and spiritual works of mercy. Of this there is little mention in very many modern "revelations". And as far as the mother of the Lord is concerned, the vision we have of her in the writings of the New Testament should be sufficient, being a vision of the apostolic faith to which we should adhere.

The principal representative of the Holy Office, Cardinal Ottaviani, wrote in the *Osservatore Romano* (4. 2. 1951): "We are not being rationalists when we warn the faithful against credulity with regard to supernatural happenings, which weaken faith in real miracles. Christ himself warned us against false prophets who would do great signs and wonders . . . . Fifty years ago one would scarcely have believed that a flood of supposed visions and miracles would excite the feelings of the faithful in many places. It was then necessary to defend the possibility of miracles; now we have to warn against credulity. We are witnessing a questionable increase in the popular passion for the miraculous. Crowds of the faithful run after supposedly

227

miraculous events and pay little heed to Christian preaching of the word. Many who do not even know the
first article of the Creed set themselves up as apostles of
an ardent 'piety'.... Disorders due to original sin manifest
themselves in the religious sphere, too, and here more
than elsewhere. Religious sentiment needs the restraint of
reason, the illumination of grace and the guidance of the
Church. Today we see strange outbreaks of religious
feeling, rejecting both reason and supernatural guidance.
The spirit of the times oscillates between blatant unbelief
and narrow, blind piety. The real Christian is constantly
aware that true religion is based on faith in Christ's Revelation which ended with the death of the apostles. We have all
we need if only we would realize it. Beyond that we need
not expect anything necessary to salvation by way of
revelations. Even the most authentic visionary experiences
cannot offer us new elements of faith and spiritual life.
True religion consists in the love of God and of our
neighbour.... Anyone who pays more heed to events of
dubious significance than to God's word, loves the world
more than God.... We must in all honesty say that the
phenomena in question may perhaps be those of natural
religion but they are not Christian and serve those as a
terrible excuse who would wish to attribute to Christianity, and especially to Catholicism, effective influences
of superstition and paganism. Why offer to the opponents
of Christianity such a spectacle of folly or unhealthy
enthusiasm?"

Not acceptable to Christians in its basic trend is the
psychological argument. I quote from the letter of a

228

disciple of C. G. Jung: "In the numerous apparitions is manifest a spiritual need which cannot be dismissed sceptically. It is symptomatic of the present situation of the Christian faith. What the Marian apparitions suggest is that Christianity, too, cannot do without the feminine element: it needs an antipole to the exclusive dominance of the male principle, as represented by the Trinity(!). The call to Mary is a call to the feminine principle and shows clearly enough that man, who in his lust for God-like powers has plunged the nations into continual catastrophes, has failed in a profound sense. The men of the Church had to recognize more than a thousand years ago at Ephesus that the Father and the Son needed a mother. We shall have to realize that man is both male and female." There are grave theological misconceptions here. We believe that in the revealed faith of the Catholic Church the emotional needs of man are sufficiently accounted for. Human needs as the basis and measure of "faith" would be nothing less than a reversal of the faith. It is God who reveals himself; it is not man who creates religion.

Discipline and proportion in Marian devotions are required also from an ecumenical point of view, that is for the sake of Christendom as a whole. We should be struck with blindness were we to overlook the implication of Jesus' legacy also in regard to the credibility of Christianity in the world. "That they too may be one in us, as thou Father, art in me, and I in thee; so that the world may come to believe that it is thou who hast sent me" (John 17:21). This is relevant to the Christian situation today. It cannot be the mind of Christ to aggravate unnecessarily the tragic separation from Protestant fellow-Christians. Any excess of devotion to Mary necessarily results in their alienation; even the best among those who in other respects are closest to the Church and most aware of the defects of their own communions are repulsed.

It is, of course, not the task of Catholic theology to "please Protestants", but simply to draw on Revelation in the spirit of the Church's tradition. Nonetheless, it would be wrong, because incompatible with the sacerdotal intentions of Jesus (as with the joint responsibility of Catholics for the origins of the division), to "write off" Christianity as a whole from our theological concerns. It would be equally wrong to see the Catholic element only in the trends of the Counter-Reformation and to misinterpret the strong emotional reactions of the Protestant world – far more effective than rational theological formulae – with pious hopes, when, for example, some converts are attracted by the Catholic devotion to Mary, whereas, in fact, the opposite is the general rule. The Catholic popular devotion to Mary was, for instance, the ultimate or penultimate obstacle to Newman's conversion.

If in our veneration of Mary there is a justified and enjoined ecumenical consideration, as there undoubtedly is, it is the consideration of maintaining a proper proportion in the spirit of the apostolic tradition. When Protestant Christians who are genuinely devout sense such a devotion to Mary among Catholic people, they begin to have confidence and to reveal their hidden longing; they are conscious of their own vacuum in this respect.

230

For many years I have had in my study a small statue of Our Lady left there for me by a friend. It has become very dear to me and has not failed to impress some of my non-Catholic visitors. Many of us may like to have similar images in our homes and it is by no means unimportant what pictures or statues we have around us. As Christians we should certainly have a meaningful mental image of Mary. We rejoice in the image of her that the New Testament shows us, in order, also in her own spirit, to give praise to the grace of God in her, the prototype of our grace. Through her and with her we make the Revelation of God's goodness and love of man in Jesus her Son the foundation of our spiritual life.

> "Hail, thou who art full of grace;
> The Lord is with thee;
> Blessed art thou among women,
> and blessed is the fruit of thy womb" (Luke 1:28, 42).

The Reunion of Christians

THERE are many people to whom the division of Christendom causes no concern, except as connected with our political tensions. They may believe in God or some divine being and try to lead decent lives. But for them the Church in the West is what they consider other forms of religion to be in other areas: all have merely a cultural, historical, or psychological significance and are useful for those people who "need" what churches offer and whom one may secretly ridicule.

Denominational differences are in their eyes the squabbles of theologians, at best a futile pastime for rational men. That the "rational man" is considered to be central, in unconscious idolatry of self and religion like poetry and beauty regarded as but a need of the human psyche, is, unconsciously as consciously, the key to this attitude. There are many others – who could count them? – who as Christians are indeed moved by the tragedy of millions of men, with a common and sincere faith in God and in Christ's redemption, being opposed to one another for centuries in suspicion and even hatred. But after many well-intentioned attempts at reconciliation, and in realistic acknowledgement of all the difficulties – dogmatic, legal and especially emotional – they are inclined to despair or resignation, considering their "idealism" a beautiful dream, an illusion like other illusions in life.

Such an attitude is, we must remind ourselves, religiously absurd – in view of the mission given by the Lord to his apostles. He enjoined unity upon them, more than spiritual unity: perfect unity embodied in his Church in order to bring about the kingdom of God in the world. It is absurd also because of the harm it does to the Christian name, tempting outsiders and those searching for truth to regard the Christian message as untrustworthy, since it represents not one message but many contradictory ones. In fact the division is such a severe handicap to the Church's power in the mission-field that to many the only solution would seem to be in minimizing to pagans the actual division between denominations and presenting it as merely differences in emphasis of the same faith.

If this were so, then the current of Christian history after a long detour throughout the intervening centuries would again be returning to its origins. For at the beginning of the division, in spite of the vehemence of the quarrel, it was precisely the declared meaning and intention of those involved not to divide the Church. The leading men of the time in spiritual and religious matters were concerned with the rethinking, purifying and

233

renewing of Christian life, with a reform the moral necessity for which is uncontested. Their one desire was to serve the kingdom of God in the name of Christ. And the others, who regarded the undertaking as dubious or wrong, wanted the same thing, to serve the kingdom of God in their way, without however uprooting so much of venerable and sacred traditions. Both parties wanted to save the Church. How then did the division, the final rift between the denominations come about?

If we look at the testimony of a competent judge like Pope Hadrian VI, who spoke from firsthand observation and experience, and compare it with the findings of modern historians of the Church such as Lortz and Jedin we shall be driven to recognize the fault on both sides in so far as the profound corruption of the late medieval Church, especially at its core, the curia of Renaissance Popes, provoked a revolt the fervour of which deteriorated into revolutionary excess.

As far as the fundamental theological ideas of the Reformation are concerned, which retain a permanent importance for their adherents, it is necessary to remember that although they contained biases, they preserved according to their intention and aim many real truths of early Christianity in their theocentric and christocentric emphasis. They were, thus, not without influence on the rejection by the Council of Trent of many widespread errors. Their propositions, even when they were in opposition to the mind of the Church at the time, served to reawaken the gospel within the one Church of Christ. Both parties were, as Möhler said, "inspired by the earnest

234

endeavour to preserve the truth, pure and unsullied Christianity". For the mass of people, even for those who were educated, it was extremely difficult, if not impossible, to form any opinion based on a deeper understanding of the far-reaching nature of the issues involved. Humanly speaking, it was pure accident, a question of circumstances or sympathies, to what party a man gave, or was forced to give, his allegiance. Only a General Council would, historically speaking, have had the competence for a real and objective settlement of the disputed questions. It never came to this for various reasons, until it was practically too late: partly because of the opposition of the Curia, which because of the notorious weakness of papal authority at the time feared the revival of old tendencies towards a conciliar supremacy; partly because of the ambiguous attitude of the reformers themselves. Thus Luther, under pressure from Eck, minimized the binding power of Councils as regards dogma by making them dependent on the testimony of the Holy Spirit, that is on his own understanding of Scripture. Yet this was not the final word on the matter. He had meanwhile appealed yet again to a General Council and in 1535 he was still explaining to the papal nuncio Vergerio his willingness to come to the Council – admittedly with arrogant conditions; but, and this was decisive for all future development, the German princes refused. Weary of disputes and disorders, they had resumed control in their own way by upholding religious order in their lands either according to the new or old ideas, as they pleased, here without bishops and

235

Mass, there supporting them, according to the principle of state authoritarianism: *Cuius regio eius religio.* The ruler decided the religion of his subjects. It was the principle of rising absolutism. Thus a completely new situation was brought about on the European Continent between 1525 and 1555 by political power. From an internal Church quarrel there grew the confrontation of two separate ecclesiastical organizations, which were mutually exclusive. According to what happened to be their own sympathies and interests, the princes appointed clergy of the old or new theology to instruct the people and lead the services, and anyone who did not conform had to leave.

In Calvin's sphere of influence the situation was similar. His theological system was notably different from that of the Lutherans. While the latter emphasized man's salvation, Calvin's vital concern was the glory of God. Election took the place of justification, that is, the first place. The Bible, the inner witness of the Holy Spirit, was given an even more exclusive significance and created religious forms with an austere community life, very different from Lutheran ardour and warmth of feeling. Yet here too, and just as much on the Catholic side, political power came to be the deciding factor and alone determined whether allegiance was given to the old or new form of Christianity. In view of all this, it is impossible to hold that membership of the body of Christ was thus settled – by men and generations who neither knew nor wanted nor could judge what was happening to them. When in 1955 the four-hundredth anniversary was held of the Lutheran religious settlement of Augsburg, Pope Pius XII expressed the wish that the road upon which divine Providence was guiding the West might prove "to lead ever closer to the lost unity". It seemed a real consolation when, in its reply, the Lutheran church assembly of Munich said that God could be relied upon, in spite of the painful division, to maintain in invisible unity all those whose desire was to serve his truth. What is really frightening for a Christian is, retrospectively, to realize the shameful fact that it was the decision of political authority, not the conscience of individuals, that guided the history of the denominations and the fate of future generations. It is right and yet only one aspect of the real facts to say that on both sides the fight was waged "only about the truth". This is certainly true of the first beginnings, of the quarrel while it was still an internal one, but its final stages were decided by the far from pure passion of the rulers for their own interests and alliances. In England successive sovereigns arbitrarily altered the country's religious adherence and, without judging individuals, there are good grounds for the view that in their measures the princes of the time were not troubled by those theological broodings and spiritual agonies which influenced the Reformers themselves. Even where the expropriation of Church property was not an enticement, it was, in general, motives which had little to do with religion that determined the course of events. The idea of freedom of conscience played no part; that was the rulers' prerogative, the people had no voice, and the theologians only in so far as they were the counsellors of princes. Through this "settlement

237

of the relations between Church and State" religion was in Germany tied to the narrow confines of the principalities. The absolute power of the State was confirmed and the State's increasingly powerful apparatus favoured an outlook in the clergy at the court and elsewhere, in which the inspiration of the spirit and the Christian ideas of freedom played only a very minor rôle. The tragi-comic side of the existence of these different denominations, as they were perpetuated from the time of the Augsburg Confession, is easily demonstrated by a few concrete examples. Only a few decades ago on a journey through the Black Forest by a round tour from Stuttgart, you would have passed more than twenty times from one sovereign territory to another and therefore from one denomination to another. Everywhere the people have for centuries been either Catholic or Protestant, because they were brought up as such – and they were brought up as such because their direction had been determined along these lines by the princes of 400 years ago. In democratic areas the same thing happened, only there the majority decision of the magistrates was the determining factor instead of the will of the ruling prince. It is true that most of these small states, both princely and democratic, were wiped off the map by Napoleon, but the confessional boundaries survived and weathered all storms up till very recently.

But now stronger forces have rendered illusory these carefully guarded outward demarcations. For a century industrial development and its effects on both working and professional classes has gradually broken down religious boundaries. Catholic refugees from East Germany have settled in Protestant villages, Protestant refugees in Catholic villages. The different denominations have been thoroughly mixed, which pleased some people and worried others. The dispositions of God take no account of our personal feelings, but we should ask ourselves how we are to understand this new situation and how we can use it for good in a true Christian spirit.

We are living in an age of intensive renewed encounter. It started first in towns and industrial areas but is now a commonplace even in the country. People are being forced to get to know one another. Earlier this was never really aimed at, but rather avoided. "Is it now after 400 years to be permitted", asked the German theologian Dr. Asmussen, "even desired, that men should get to know one another at the level of what each holds most sacred?" According to psychological laws (which we cannot circumvent by miracles) it is indeed a first prerequisite for that union of the faithful desired and commanded by the Lord that we should get to know one another. How otherwise is any spiritual rapprochement, to say nothing of a return to unity even conceivable? It is, therefore, indubitably one of the first and most important religious duties, especially for educated Christians, clergy and laity, who live among those of different beliefs, that together with their own faith received through upbringing, they should acquire an understanding, as impartial as possible, of the separated denominations. It would be self-deception to suppose that we have such an understanding already from our religious instruction in our own faith – in rare cases this may be so, but in general not, or at least not knowledge in love and impartiality, the essential prerequisites.

What it comes down to is an appreciation of our fundamental union in Christ as well as of the more or less important points of difference. There is already a considerable literature which is of great value in this respect, for example the writings of W. H. van de Pol, Lambert, Henry St. John, Yves Congar.

In Germany where there was a common pressure in the Nazi era on both denominations this certainly acted as an opportune preparation for encounter. The set-backs are almost all conditioned by non-theological, political factors. As Christians we cannot face one another merely negatively when we live together, sharing the same fate, in a world of moral and religious collapse and de-christianization, in which so many are indifferent or antagonistic towards Christianity. This does not mean that the differences between denominations are removed, but that we now see them in a different light from that in which earlier generations saw them. Admittedly the age of Enlightenment smoothed over these antagonisms, but no true Christian would desire this "solution". It is no longer a question of choosing a rational religion, but of faith or unbelief. In the fundamentals of the Christian belief in God in the name of Christ, the incarnate Lord and Redeemer, in the communion of prayer and love, Christians know themselves to be on the same side, and the nearer they are to the one Lord, the nearer they are to one another.

We are faced with the question how to help those spiritually who from their ordinary social contacts have gained the wish to get to know one another better, without being drawn into conflicts because of loyalty to tradition. They feel themselves impelled, in so far as it is in their power, to contribute something to the spiritual rapprochement between Christians. It will be clear already that this has nothing to do with political considerations, but is a purely religious desire on the part of very many Christians. It hardly needs to be said that mixed marriages are no ideal solution. The Catholic partner because of his stronger links with the Church faces difficulties of conscience in the matter of possible concessions concerning the upbringing of the children; the exclusion from the sacraments which ensues in such a case is a spiritual burden that can easily be fatal to the marriage.

It would be an incalculable gain for the cause of Christianity, in the overcoming of old grievances, and a triumph, a real miracle for the spirit of truth and love, if the leading representatives of the different denominations could agree to ensure that the textbooks used in schools for religious instruction gave our growing youth a true picture of the other faith. In other words, the sections on the doctrine, history and culture of the other denominations should be printed from a text approved by them. Useful, too, are discussions of such problems in groups within each denomination, for instance groups of the so-called lay apostolate. But this presupposes direction by a theologian of sound knowledge and ecumenical disposition, and at present there are not many who have more than an

241

average knowledge of the relevant questions. They first have to be taught, perhaps in university courses for a select group of younger priests and laymen. It is clear that none of this can be accomplished without theological guidance.

A further and, in a certain sense, ideal solution, but unfortunately only a partial one and only practicable in towns, is the formation of ecumenical groups, such as the Una Sancta groups in Germany. There are two types of these, one composed exclusively of theologians, the other with the participation of lay people with the support of theologians; the meetings are being held with an equal number of participants of each denomination. Such groups have been authorized by Rome, provided the diocesan bishop's approval has also been given. That the Holy See does not take part in the conferences of the World Council of Churches (the possibility remains open) should be understood. But that the Church welcomes the ecumenical cause is shown by her positive attitude towards the groups mentioned above, which meet for conversation and communal prayer at regular intervals, exclusively for the purpose of getting to know one another better, of studying controversial questions in papers and lectures, and of consulting one another in a brotherly spirit on concerns which affect the various denominations. It is understood that the participants are to regard one another as equal partners in the conversation, as the *instructio* of the Holy Office emphasizes. Here it is implicitly stated, that the Catholic partners have something to gain from the meeting as well as the Protestant, that Catholic participants do not have to regard themselves solely as giving, nor the Protestants solely as receiving. This corresponds to the experiences of the participants. The aim is not to make conversions, but to sustain the spiritual conditions in which a more profound spiritual encounter can flourish, in order to come nearer to one another in Christ – to listen to one another and learn from one another without unworthy compromises, but in truth, sincerity and readiness. For such bridges between denominations to be possible and to exist without putting the participants in a false position *vis-à-vis* their own church, it is essential that the meetings are between sincere Catholics and Protestants, who have as their common basis the Revelation in Christ in the sense of the old ecumenical Councils. The cordial, brotherly spirit of such meetings is exceedingly heartening, but any bigger movement is not to be expected, at least until a sufficient number of intellectually well-prepared theologians is available on both sides, who can offer some guarantee of fruitful development; and at the moment there are too few of them even to equal the number of laity who would be ready and willing for such work. Compared with the situation in the past much has been achieved already if such meetings can now take place in the larger towns – the future lies in God's hand.

When we consider our traditional religious education we must admit that it is far from adequate to meet the present situation of religious pluralism and indeed questionable in itself. On both sides the faithful have been brought up from youth not only as Christians in the spirit of their denomination, but in opposition to one another, and with notions of the other side which are in general noticeably far removed from justice and love. This was perhaps done in good faith and with the good intention of safeguarding the sheep. But what we do not respect, we cannot love; what we do not love, we are not in a position to know in truth. Distortion is the result, and in the course of time many people become aware that something is amiss. They will draw their conclusions in their own way, some in this manner, some in another. What Christians ought to achieve above all is to think well of one another, ("Do to other men all that you would have them do to you . . .") realize the mystical and real power of baptism and prayer, and so honour the fundamental bond with the body of Christ in others too. It is true that many Protestants as well as many born Catholics live according to the rules of worldly wisdom and possess little more than an inkling of what Christianity is; they are aware only that Christ lived, that for some there is the Pope and that others support the Reformers, without themselves belonging or wishing to belong to either side. But in the case of many – of whom the participants in ecumenical circles are only a fraction – one constantly discovers how deep and genuine is their spirit of faith, prayer and love of their neighbour. Seen as a whole, more of the substance of faith has probably been preserved in Catholic countries and areas, although we too have to contend with much deplorable indifference and apostasy. In spite of the greater unity of Catholicism, the sad fact is that certain so-called Catholic countries are, like the Protestant ones, in fact more like mission areas.

244

What might bring about a deepening and renewal of the Christian spirit would be precisely the spiritual rapprochement of the faithful remainder of the separated parts of Christianity. First of all, we must shut from our minds and our hearts all unkindness and unfairness and it must be binding on the conscience of both partners that they listen honestly to the concerns of those who are looking for unity. Only then will the great scandal cease which Christianity now presents to the world, when unbelievers can complain that they could not very well be expected to examine the greater right of one party in order then to join the best! Any genuine concern for mutual brotherliness undertaken by both sides in personal piety, with a sincere conscience, with integrity and penance, is in every respect in accordance with the mind of Christ.

It is far from being generally acknowledged that we Catholics have amends to make too. Because of our consciousness of possessing the values of salvation in an ideal integrity and completeness, we tend to hide from ourselves and attempt to veil from others the historical loss which we for our part suffered, with regard to the realization of those values, through a one-sided defensive attitude towards Protestant ideas. Think only of the great efforts needed to restore the Bible as handbook and guide for people and even clergy, not because of mere laziness but precisely because this is a Protestant concern, though ultimately one of the early Church. We cannot, therefore, in honesty think that the prejudices are all on the Protestant side – although they have many too. We ourselves need to do penance also for certain

245

aberrations in the sphere of religious instruction. For us, surrounded by the richness of Catholicism, it is not a question of a "fragmentary existence as a church", as a convert said of Protestantism. The question is, as Bishop Besson said, whether we too do not need to think in terms of a "conversion", as regards the essential nature of many of our *dévotionettes* and the order of values presented in our religious instruction. Even those who are most sympathetic towards us in these ecumenical dialogues ask again and again – and in fact not without reason – whether the balance of the vital tension in Catholicism between authority and conscience, which was considered by Newman to be an essential element in the life of the Church, is not actually very much weighted in favour of the earthly external and legalistic aspects. Moreover, if faith appears above all to be a matter of assenting to clauses in an ideological system, of a relationship to definite concepts, and moral doctrines give the impression that it is obedience to legal rules which is all-important, instead of emphasizing inner harmony with the holy will of God, then danger arises that the real core of faith in the life of the soul, a personal relationship with God, complete devotion to him in co-operation with Jesus Christ (the one essential for salvation), will be completely obscured.

Michael de la Bedoyère has once admitted that, although he was brought up in a devout Catholic family and in an exceptionally favourable environment, it was more than fifty years before he grasped the deeper meaning of his religion and he surmises that for many it must be even more difficult. He thought that the fatal defect of our average religious instruction was to make religion look like a sort of moral code, a discipline to enforce adherence to a mass of doctrines, rules and external pious practices. This resulted in our interior attention being distracted from its focal point to peripheral issues and the heart of the matter, the relationship to God through and with Jesus Christ, being neglected. We could no longer see the wood for the trees and were led round and round the real essential instead of directly to it. It was because of this that those outside the Church, who consciously or unconsciously were seeking the meaning of life and the right way, could not find the way to the Church. It is to be feared that Count de la Bedoyère is only too right. We must, therefore, be truly grateful to God if the simple, roughly drawn theocentric line of Protestant piety restores to us something that is not "Protestant" but in fact part of the biblical and early Christian life of faith. It is heartening to find a Catholic layman who is aware of all this.

That the different denominations have a common basis is undeniable: through Christ to God. It is true that there is a certain one-sidedness in Luther's christology. When in one of his bold images he speaks of the human nature of the Lord, as "God's grub", we might wonder whether the Word really became flesh. For it is surely Christ's humanity, which redeemed us through obedience to the Father's will, which now, sitting at the right hand of God, acts as mediator for us all. We must not lay to the charge of the whole of Protestant Christianity an obscure theological interpretation on the part of Luther,

247

since leading Protestant theologians in any case follow the Council of Chalcedon. There is too a certain trend in Catholic piety which has caused Karl Rahner, for example, to recall and emphasize the fact that in Jesus Christ God took on human nature, so that "Jesus Christ, who is a man" (1 Tim. 2:5), is redeemer and mediator in his solidarity with us. God redeemed us not through himself but through this man, in whom the Word was made flesh. There is still much to do before the truth of the epistle to the Hebrews and the liturgy about Christ as our mediator in heaven is once again clearly reintegrated into the consciousness and piety of the Catholic faithful.

Thus a new encounter between earnest Christians, who wish to serve the kingdom of God and who possess some intellectual qualities can bring only blessings to the Church. The opportunities for a fruitful exchange with non-Catholic Christians do, however, vary according to their objective theological closeness to us and the degree of spiritual readiness. It is not possible to regard Protestant-ism as an inner union like that of the Catholic Church, although the tendencies towards unity are present and growing. It would be very shortsighted of us, too, to speak with a kind of self-satisfaction of the "disintegration" of Protestantism and to feel pleased at the problems of the movement towards unity within Protestantism. In fact anything which involves a real loss to Protestant Christian-ity is also a loss for the common Christian cause against disbelief, for the substitute is not the Church but nihilism; and any inner strengthening of the evangelical elements within Protestantism is a gain for Christianity as a whole and even, indirectly, for the Church. It would be a good thing if Christians today could learn "to think big" and include in their love and prayers all who are brothers in Christ, even though we can all only serve the kingdom of God in one place, to which God has called us through his grace. The real conflict of views between the denominations lies in their understanding of what the Church is: are we through baptism already members of the body of Christ, of the communion of saints, enjoying the life of grace, as Catholics believe; or is the Church only an "event" made actual in faith by those who gather together in Christ's name, which is the Protestant view? Do the sacred offices, priesthood and sacraments act as channels for the presence of Christ through the Spirit (Catholic) or does everything depend upon the act of faith, through which individuals are justified and meet one another in charismatic brotherhood (Protestant)? All this is accentuated by the problem of the apostolic succession and the primacy of the Petrine chair throughout the ages. Here one can sense again and again the real crux of ecumenical endeavours. For this reason it seems unduly optimistic for von Balthasar in his excellent book on Karl Barth to suggest that if once the barrier existing on such questions as creation and redemption, nature and grace, were down or at least less penetrable, then there would be no further important difficulties for Protestants in the sphere of ecclesiology. Karl Barth himself is an example of how the matter really stands. He is close to the Catholic thinking on creation and redemption, but nonetheless – for Christ's sake as he thinks – considers the Pope to be Anti-christ.

249

It is precisely in regard to the hierarchical order of the Church that the obstacles are far from purely theological. For theologians too are men with unconscious psychological influences – here it is especially the fear, which is historically and psychologically easy to understand, that they would with uncanny certainty fall into the clutches of the "Roman system", a sublime "spiritual dictatorship"; and this fear holds at bay even those who through their biblical studies have traced the bases of the sacred office to the New Testament. There are also, of course, all sorts of misconceptions (nourished by weaknesses in the Catholic reality) about the spiritual rather than earthly character of authority, about the relationship between primacy and episcopacy, and the whole people of faith. For the people should not form a passive church of "hearers", but be aware of their rôle as co-responsible workers for the kingdom of God, just as the bishops are not passive tools of his Holiness, the Pope's "echo", as has been suggested, but draw their responsibility from the apostles themselves, though in union with the centre that is Peter. It has been said that Luther would not have started out on the road to Protestantism if he had had to deal with Popes such as the Church has been blessed with in recent times. This is easy to believe – but irrelevant: we must accept God's dispositions and judgments as they are and have faith in their significance for our salvation.

In their zeal to defend the primacy some writers have been tempted not to put the same emphasis on its correlate of episcopal and lay responsibility. For them a consideration of what G. Dejaifve S. J. [1]says may be useful: "Nothing was altered (by the First Vatican Council) in the organic constitution of the Church and in particular in the collegiate order of the ecclesiastical hierarchy." Admittedly there resulted in practice, he adds, an involuntary bias because of difficult circumstances; the Council could not be brought to a close, but only adjourned. As a consequence its definitions are an authentic sketch of the constitution of the Church but only from one aspect – an important one but not the only one. For to define the head is not to define the body. In the second issue of *Irénikon* in 1956 there was printed a very important document issued by the German bishops in 1875. It is unfortunately not included in Denzinger and is very little known. In contradiction to Bismarck's statement that the State had no longer to deal with independent and responsible bishops but merely with executors of the papal will, they explain, with the solemn corroboration of Pius IX, that the Pope has a *potestas suprema, ordinaria* and *immediata,* but that the statement that this is a *potestas illimitata* and that, by virtue of his infallibility in *ex cathedra* decisions, he is an absolute sovereign, is based on a completely false conception. "According to the teaching of the Catholic Church the Pope is Bishop of Rome, not bishop of any other town or diocese.... He cannot change the constitution given the Church by her divine founder.... The episcopacy exists by virtue of that same divine institution on which the papacy is based: it too has its rights and duties and it owes

---

[1] *Nouvelle Revue théologique* (1952).

251

them to that disposition provided by God himself, which the Pope has neither the right nor the power to alter. It is, therefore, a complete misunderstanding of the Vatican decision to think that through it episcopal jurisdiction has been assimilated into the papal jurisdiction ... and that the bishops are merely the tools of the Pope."

In view of all these difficulties caution as well as hopefulness must be observed in speaking of the possibilities and prospects of ecumenical development. In Protestantism we are faced with not one but many dogmatic systems, which differ among themselves, yet have a profound unity, since they are bound together by certain ways of thoughts and basic feelings of spirituality which are very different from those of Catholics. In many respects it has still not been settled to what extent there is room and a home for evangelical elements within the Mother Church, as the phrase "there are many dwelling-places in my Father's house" suggests there should be, nor is this within the competence of the individual to judge, but must be left to the authority of the Church. Much is possible today which would have been impossible half a century ago – surely then what seems impossible now will be possible to God in the future? We must remember that although the Council of Trent condemned certain extreme formulations, it did not draw up against the reformers a Catholic system of the truth of Revelation (it abided instead by the conciliar tradition); for its part the reformed theology drew up articles of faith, but without intending or being able to endow them with dogmatic binding power like an ecumenical Council. It should be clear from this that much that is important has been left open and is in a state of flux. As we know, there are two main schools of thought within the World Council of Churches, and the Amsterdam conference called the one "Catholic" and the other "Protestant". To the Catholic type, according to this definition which is measured by the yardstick of the apostolic succession, belong the Anglican and Orthodox churches, as well as the Roman Catholic Church. At the present time, however, there are strong tendencies towards Catholicism on biblical grounds within the Protestant church on the Continent, particularly in so far as the typically Protestant view that faith alone is necessary is beginning to give way to a broader more Catholic view. This has its roots in the incarnation of God and so embraces the whole act of salvation. It is a new discovery which is leading to a more profound and serious attitude towards the creation, the visible Church with her offices and sacraments, the importance of tradition for an understanding of Scripture, and man's responsibility in grace. For the advocates of this basically Catholic outlook there is no question of a dichotomy between word and sacrament, Scripture and tradition, charism and office, grace and human effort, but instead a vital polarity. And as far as the different types of thought and ways of approaching spirituality are concerned, the question remains open of whether what seems to be in contradiction while a state of separation exists, might not appear within Catholic unity as a natural variation of living in the Holy Spirit. For surely this is the significance of such opposite intellectual and spiritual types, as Paul and James, as the Jewish and Hellenic forms of Christianity, not excluding one another but fusing together. The fundamental feeling of the Protestant Christian that he lives by grace alone does not exclude individual responsibility, the will prepared in him by the Lord, the surrender of the heart. Yet many converts who know their theology find no contradiction in living according to this "evangelical" idea within the Catholic Church. Such examples seem like a hopeful sign of what would be possible if the ecumenical dialogue were to be developed to an authoritative form at the highest level.

We have one historical precedent when in the eighteenth century Pope Innocent XI gave his support to the talks on union in Hanover between Spinola and Molanus with which the philosopher G. W. Leibniz was closely connected.[2] Plans were drawn up and circulated in the European courts which amounted to a suggestion that the dispositions of the Council of Trent – which had of necessity taken its decisions without the collaboration of the reformed theologians – were capable of amendment by the contributions of Protestant theologians – in the same way as at the time of Arianism, the decisions of earlier Councils were supplemented by the addenda of new Councils in consequence of new problems. Abortive as these endeavours proved after a few years, partly due to Bossuet's

---

[2] The best examination of this question is G. J. Jordan's *The Reunion of the Churches,* A Study of G. W. Leibniz and his great attempt (London, 1927); cf. G. Molanus, *Regulae circa Christianorum omnium ecclesiasticum unionem* (1683); G. W. Leibniz, *Systema theologicum;* Bossuet, *Œuvres* XXV (Versailles, 1817), p. 205.

intervention and to the background of French politics, they were not entirely in vain; they deepened the conviction that God's spirit was still to some extent in evidence among those separated by particular need and by political power, and that much which in separation seems to be in opposition could in fact in the living unity within the Mother Church prove to be fruitful. As van de Pol points out, the present separation does not mean that the Catholic Church has to disdain Christian witness, which is borne and taught, prayed and lived by those of Protestant faith and is founded on Scripture. He quotes with approval the opinion of both von Balthasar and Asmussen that the Catholic Church and Protestant Christians have hardly begun to establish contact with one another at any really profound level. Many more truly spiritual efforts are needed, much patience "in truth and love", many more prayers and sacrifices on the part of Christ's meek sheep, who in Carmel (and other convents) or as Protestant deaconesses offer up "for the sake of his body, the Church" all that they suffer in union with the afflictions of Christ (Col. 1:24). Only when these are forthcoming will diversity and unity be sufficiently illuminated and the now sanctified remainder of those once separated find themselves reunited in Christ, while Antichrist gathers together his hosts – for the Last Judgment.